To Sharon —
With all my (?
and deep (?

Larry (?
Psalm 22:28

KINGDOM
Life

Finding Life
Beyond Church

LARRY BURDEN

Tulsa, Oklahoma

KINGDOM LIFE
© 2009 by Larry Burden

Published by Insight Publishing Group
8801 S. Yale, Suite 410
Tulsa, OK 74137
918-493-1718

Unless otherwise noted, all Scripture quotations are taken from the *Holy Bible: New King James Version*, © 1979, 1980, 1982 by Thomas Nelson, Inc., Publishers. Scripture quotations marked KJV are taken from the Kings James Version. Scripture quotations marked NIV are from the *New International Version*, © 1960, 1962, 1963, 1968, 1971, 1972, 1973, 1975, 1977, 1995 by The Lockman Foundation. Used by permission.

The names of some individuals and places have been changed for privacy reasons.

ISBN: 978-1-932503-83-8
Library of Congress catalog card number: 2009922343

Printed in the United States of America

There's a nasty little secret known by most church-going people…something's wrong, something's not quite right, it's not really working like we say it is. Man's system of doing church isn't working how God intended it to. Larry Burden's groundbreaking new book *Kingdom Life* shows us a much more excellent way…God's way. Through invaluable personal experience, insightful Bible teaching and memorable ideas, Pastor Burden shows how every believer and church can discover God's kingdom way of change, growth, and influence. I highly recommend this book.

—John Mason
Author of *An Enemy Called Average* and numerous other best-selling books

◆   ◆   ◆

God is doing church in a different way! He is creating a new wineskin that will reflect the heart of the Lord for this generation. God's heart is for His kingdom to be established in the earth. *Kingdom Life* reveals a journey that transitions Larry Burden from a traditional mind-set to a powerful kingdom paradigm! As a young man, Larry was disappointed with the poverty he saw in the ministry. The call of God on his life was rejected for years as he chose a more prosperous professional career.

Years later, after surrendering his life to the Lord and accepting the position of a church pastor, Larry found himself trapped in a system of impossibilities. A life filled with extremes in the various systems of church life resulted in a life-changing encounter with the Lord. Your life will also be changed as you walk with Larry through the transition he made from building man's kingdom to building the kingdom of God. *Kingdom Life* will cause you to walk out of old religious systems and embrace the new wineskin of the kingdom of God. I highly recommend this book for all believers who are hungry for a fresh move of the Holy Spirit!

—Barbara Wentroble
Author, and Founder of International
Breakthrough Ministries

◆ ◆ ◆

Pastor Larry Burden defines a reality that plagues far too many Western churches. It is an undermining factor that manifests through the misapplication of what should be operating as gifts within the church. Instead, the "pastor system" and the "training system" he describes have stymied the Body maturity needed for a vibrant, overcoming, and transforming church. Yet, his profound and enlightening insights go beyond the identification of the problem. With examples from his own journey as a pastor and church builder, he outlines the liberating discovery that has reset his own course through the central theme of Jesus' message of the kingdom of God. The core truth he unfolds in *Kingdom Life*, that every church and ministry leader ought to be applying, is a practical kingdom-church model that is unveiled in an anointed and penetrating reexamination of Ezekiel's wheel.

—Morris Ruddick
Founder, Global Initiatives Foundation

◆ ◆ ◆

While truly serving God, Larry Burden has come from a life of despair to kingdom of God living in victory, joy, and peace. He shares from his heart a powerful message, proving the eternal truth that when we operate in Christ's love, that love will never fail in any area of our life. You will rejoice and weep as your own life is mirrored in the knowledge, wisdom, and understanding of *Kingdom Life*. With excitement and expectation, you will cherish each word of this book that brings forth God's kingdom revelation to a hungry and needy heart.

—Bobbie Jean Merck
Founder/President, A Great Love Ministries

♦ ♦ ♦

Kingdom Life is the story of an amazing journey from a dead religious system to the profound discovery of God's dominion, authority, and power. Pastor Larry Burden has crossed a new horizon in his quest to move from the mediocrity of "church as usual" to actually carrying and extending the spiritual government of God in the earth. This book will show you how to transition from the congregational to the congressional and from the religious to a passion-filled relationship with the Creator of the universe.

—Dr. Don Crum
Founder, Leadership International

♦ ♦ ♦

I invite you to read this book about the journey of Pastor Larry Burden and the revelation received. You will step into the world of the kingdom of God and be changed forever. Like Noah, Pastor Burden suddenly found himself going beyond a man-made system and receiving revelation to build after the model of heaven.

—Tricia Miller
President, Miller International Ministries, Inc.

♦ ♦ ♦

In Pastor Larry's new book entitled *Kingdom Life,* he brings out the true heart, passion, and inspiration of "Kingdom-Principle-Living." This book is a must read for every pastor and full-time minister.

—Russell M. Plilar
Senior Pastor, Seedtime & Harvest Church

DEDICATION

To Kathy—for your love and faithfulness to follow and serve alongside me through more than thirty-five years of marriage and twenty years of ministry. Apart from Jesus, you are the greatest gift and joy of my life.

To Brandon and Willy, Matt and Liane—no father could be more proud of his sons and daughters. Thank you for beautiful grandchildren. You have brought indescribable joy to Mom and me and you are the greatest treasures of our lives. Thank you for always loving and standing with us no matter the circumstance.

To Marco and Val—for adopting Kathy and me and receiving our family into your hearts and home. You are our special son and daughter. No one has taught us more about the importance of "family" than you. Thank you for standing in the gap for Brandon and Matt. I am forever grateful!

To David and Linda—your love and support is recorded in the heart of the Father. Thank you for helping Kathy and me navigate through the challenges of life and for being there for us as we continue to build God's kingdom. You have captured our hearts.

To Steve and DeeAnne—for teaching me in word and deed how to walk in love and grace. No one exhibits this more than you; thank you for being there for Kathy and me and the Kingdom Life family. We are better people because of your influence. Your children mirror your excellence of spirit, character, and devotion to Jesus.

To Mel, Barbara, and Shirley—for investing your time and hearts into Kathy and me and teaching us the more excellent ways of the Father. Thank you for the hours of prayer and godly counsel. The fruit of your labors will only be fully known in heaven.

To Marcelita—you are a constant source of strength and counsel. I pray that your dreams become reality as you continue to place your hand to the plow, never looking back. Thank you for loving Kathy and me and walking with us through the years. We love you.

To Ken and Dorothy—for carrying me in the Spirit, especially during the formative years. Few would have remained as faithful as you to see the completion of the assignment. I am forever grateful. You are the rock of your family.

To Apostles Jim and Jean—for receiving our family into yours and for parenting us with such love and affirmation. You are the most honorable ministers I have ever known. You brought us back, and I can never thank you enough.

To the Kingdom Life family—for believing in the vision and serving with Kathy and me as we have endeavored to build the kingdom of God together. You are a family of ministers, and it is a privilege to serve with such honorable "kings." We love you beyond words!

To Mom and Dad, Hobart and Jean—the last are first. Thank you for helping us along the way of life and for always being there when we needed you most. You have been a constant source of stability. What can we say except, "Thank you; we love you deeply." Dad, I miss you still.

CONTENTS

We live in a time when the church is in major transition. The 21st century has arrived and the Body of Christ around the world is experiencing revolutionary change!

Some are endeavoring to deny this change. Some are embracing it and others are trying to define it. Nevertheless, change is here and it is here to stay!

This volume, written by my good friend, Pastor Larry Burden, addresses the critical questions and issues of change in the Body of Christ.

The major changes the church is experiencing today are primarily structural. Dr. C. Peter Wagner introduced the term, New Apostolic Reformation, to describe the current change in the church. This helps us to understand that the changes we need are biblical and reformational. They are not cosmetic changes such as altering our worship styles or putting new names on old things. These changes are based on the Word of God and they are as potentially impacting as the Reformation led by Martin Luther and others in 16th century Europe. Wagner points out that the Reformation then was primarily about doctrine; the current reformation is about restructuring the church and bringing her into alignment with the original apostolic pattern (See I Corinthians 12:28).

You will read in this book about the key areas where the church needs to undergo reformation. The first area is transitioning the church into a kingdom mind-set. The church has been too focused on itself and therefore needs a revelation of the kingdom of God. A "four walls" mentality has hindered the Body of Christ from pursuing God's kingdom agenda in every sphere of life. After all, the kingdom transcends the church. The church is a part of the kingdom, but the kingdom is God's rule and reign over everything—over heaven, over earth, over angels, over nations, over civil rulers, and over the church.

The second area of reformation moves the church from a family-only mentality to an army mentality. Scripturally, the church is both family and army. But too often we remain family and never become an army to engage the enemies of the Gospel who war against the will of God being done on earth as it is in heaven. This area relates to the training of the people of God to fulfill the ministry the Lord has called them to in the workplace, in the home, in the schoolhouse or wherever. Every saint is called to be a worker and warrior in the Spirit.

This book covers a heavy topic in a very readable way. The author weaves scriptural truths through an autobiographical tapestry. You will be reading his exciting stories when suddenly you will be hit with an important truth.

This volume will challenge the Body of Christ and you, as a follower of Christ, to change. It will also provide you the inspiration and instruction needed for divinely directed change.

—Jim Hodges
Founder/President, Federation of Ministers
and Churches International

ACKNOWLEDGEMENTS

Deepest thanks to my son Brandon Burden for the hours spent laboring over this book. Thank you for taking the initiative to write it. Thank you for "holing up" with me for days to hear and write the story. Thank you for the insight of the story line. Thank you for typing until you were exhausted. Thank you for the hours of poring over the edits and revising the manuscript. Thank you for insisting that the final work demonstrate excellence. Without you, this project would have never been completed. I love you, son.

Special thanks to Linda Mason for the outstanding job of copyediting and to Karen Griffin for the excellent final review of the manuscript. Your tenacity, skill, eye for detail, and loving heart are deeply appreciated.

The best lessons in life are learned by experience. After thirty-seven years of Christian service, twenty of those in pastoral ministry, I have seen church splits, moral failures, leadership abuse, manipulation and control, Jezebel spirits, churches become cults, and systems inspired more by man than God. Life in the church is quite an experience. It might even make a good reality television program if it were not so disgraceful.

The church in America is in a critical hour. We have some of the largest churches in the world, yet we are making very little impact on American culture. We have digressed from a church that was once the center of society, the standard for moral living, and the voice of culture to one that is today of little influence. The world no longer listens to the church or cares what she has to say. To many, she is irrelevant, unimportant, and unnecessary.

The church today is much like a dream a friend of mine once told me. In this dream, my friend was driving down a freeway when he got stuck behind a large box truck. The truck was heavily loaded down with gear and was literally creeping along. Behind it crawled a long line of cars, none of which could seem to get around the truck. Frustrated with the situation, he called out to the Lord and asked Him what he should do. Firmly, the Lord said, "Well, move over to the next lane!" So he moved over, and when he did, the cars behind him followed. The Lord then revealed that the box truck was the church system he was stuck in, and God was instructing him to move out of it.

I believe that pastors and church attendees today are much like my friend in the dream. We are stuck in systems that are weighted down with a heavy load, and we have slowed down to a snail's pace. We are trying to pick up speed and change the world around us before it swallows us up, but we can't seem to see around the truck that is in front of us. Something is desperately wrong. We need to change lanes and shift gears.

Thus, the purpose for this book. Over the past twenty years, I have helped build three successful churches, two of which eventually collapsed. Not fully understanding why these churches failed, I set out to uncover the reason. During this process, God granted me insight into the systems by which the churches were built—systems only partially functional at best. As I reflected upon and examined these systems, I decided to call them the *pastor system* and the *training system*.

In this book, I will reveal the dynamics of each of these systems and why they have failed the American church. I will also present a kingdom church model that I believe has the potential to bring true change to the body of Christ and bless our nation.

It is my prayer that as you read this book, whether as a pastor, an individual, or as part of a group, you will identify with the pastor and training systems and be encouraged as you find your fit in the kingdom of God. Maybe you are stuck behind the slow-moving box truck, unable to reach your destiny in Christ. The good news is that you do not have to stay there. There is a way out, and God has provided the answer for you.

CHAPTER ONE

THE GLORY DAYS

"I'm moving you. Don't resist."

"What?" I thought. "What do You mean, 'I'm moving you?'"

Fear gripped my heart and panic swept over my mind. I knew God was speaking loud and clear, but what was He trying to say? It's all over? Seven years down the tubes? What I've sacrificed and given my entire life for is finished?

God didn't seem to budge. "I'm moving you. Don't resist."

The words sank deep into my heart. I began to worry.

For seven years, I had served as the associate pastor of a metropolitan California church and life had been great. I had traveled internationally, meeting many of the foremost leaders of the body of Christ, while at the same time getting to pastor one of the fastest-growing churches in America.

My position at this church, World Shakers Christian Center, had begun in the fall of 1993. It was a brand-new church at the time and the senior pastor, John, had approached me about becoming his associate pastor. Fresh out of Bible college, I was more than ecstatic to jump at the opportunity.

For years, I had prayed, "God, I just want to change the world. Use me for Your purpose. Use me for Your glory. Let me make a difference in the world."

My heart had yearned for so long to be a part of something greater than myself. I had cried out for God to place me where He wanted me, and just like that, my prayers were finally answered.

I recalled my first assignment as associate pastor. Lester Sumrall was coming to town, and I was asked to drive him to the airport in time to catch his flight. Someone had already warned me that Dr. Sumrall didn't like to be asked a lot of questions so I should keep them to a minimum. New on the job, I was a nervous wreck by the time I picked him up.

Here is the man of God, I thought, *God's man of faith and power, a nation shaker, a history maker, the man who spent countless hours with Smith Wigglesworth himself. This is the man who cast the demons out of Carlita, the possessed Filipino girl, and made her whole again! And I'm taking this guy to the airport? That's just great.*

Knowing that Dr. Sumrall did not tolerate tardiness, I arrived fifteen minutes early to pick him up. He got in the car and we took off for the airport. He sat in the front seat, his cold, steel eyes penetrating my very soul.

Then came question after question. "Where are you from? Are you married? Do you have children? How many? Boys or girls?"

Sweat popped out on my forehead. I fumbled for the answers, "Texas. Yes. Yes. Two. Boys."

The answers seemed to escape my mind. Seconds stretched into hours, minutes into days. *How fast can this car go?* I thought. *Just get me out of here.*

Dr. Sumrall didn't stop. "What brought you to California? Where do you plan to pastor long term? Will you continue to help John pastor this church?"

My goodness, will he ever stop? What does he want with me? Does he see a devil in me? Why is this guy analyzing my life? God, if you'll just get me out of this car, I promise I'll do anything.

I knew if I messed up and said the wrong answer this guy was going to think that Pastor John hired a yo-yo. *They certainly didn't teach me how to handle Dr. Sumrall in Bible school*, I thought to myself.

We finally arrived at the airport. I was never so glad. Dr. Sumrall's cold eyes pierced me once again. He took my hand.

"Let's pray," he said. "Father, I thank You for this man You have brought here to be a part of this ministry. Thank You for training him, equipping him, and anointing him. I pray blessing over him today in the name of Jesus. I break the power of all discouragement that would try to come and buffet him. I stand against it in Jesus' name and I pray that he will fulfill his destiny and his purpose successfully in Jesus' name. Amen."

He then looked at me and said, "Son, be successful. Whatever you set your hand to do, be successful." The door opened and he hopped out.

"I'M MOVING YOU. DON'T RESIST."

I never forgot that experience. As one of the greatest prayers that any man of God had ever prayed over my life, I could still feel the anointing in it as I remembered it now, several years later.

Again, my mind snapped to. "I'm moving you. Don't resist."

"But God," I argued, "what am I going to do? All I know is the pastorate. Are you taking this church away from me?"

God's peace calmed my mind. I knew He was up to something, but I had no clue what. All I had known for the past seven years was megaministry. It had become a part of my life, a part of my mind-set, and a part of my philosophy.

What am I going to do now? I thought to myself.

I had to get ready for service, so I finished shaving. It was a beautiful California Sunday morning, and I was on my way to church—my church—or at least it still felt like it was my church. Eight hundred church members were waiting for me that morning.

God, what am I going to tell them? Good-bye? See you later? I'm no longer your pastor? I wish you the best? God, why are You doing this to me? You're messing up my plan. I'm called to pastor a megachurch. You brought me here from Texas. You changed my life. You put me in this position. Now you're taking it away from me?

My mind drifted back to the day Norvel Hayes came to town. I had been associate pastor for about a year and had pretty much figured out how the system worked. Guest speakers would come to town, I would take them from meeting to meeting, and then they would go on their way. I had it down perfectly, so I figured Norvel would be no different.

I was never further from the truth. Norvel was like no one else I had ever met. He was not your ordinary run-of-the-mill minister of the Gospel. Businessman turned evangelist, he was world renowned for his deliverance ministry, and he was powerfully anointed.

On this particular night as I hosted, a very dear lady flew in from the state of Florida to attend the meeting. She was diagnosed with several major medical diseases and was struggling to live. I remembered as they brought her in and sat her behind me on the second row. Norvel had finished preaching an outstanding message as he usually does and had just transitioned into the ministry time. He announced to the crowd that a very special lady had flown in all the way from Florida to receive her miracle, and he called her out of the audience to the front of the auditorium.

"Now people, we're going to pray for this woman tonight," he said. "We're going to lay hands on her and pray for God to touch her, heal her, and make her completely whole in Jesus' name."

Then Norvel reached out, laid his hands on her cheeks, and said, "Lord Jesus, I ask You to just touch this lady and heal her and make her whole in Jesus' name. Amen."

Immediately, the woman fell to the ground and her head lay right at my feet. It looked like nothing was happening as she stayed completely still for about fifteen seconds. Suddenly, her head tilted backward, her mouth opened, and a shriek erupted from her unlike anything I had ever heard. The sound exploded in my ears and made the hair on the back of my neck stand up. I watched in shock at what happened next. This sickly, fragile woman began to flop like a fish across the floor. She rolled to the left, and then back to the right, shrieking all the while. I had never seen anything like this in my entire life. I wondered if this woman would even come out of this thing alive.

Norvel began to chuckle at the sight. "Don't be afraid. Don't let the devil steal your peace. The demons are leaving her and God is just healing her," he said to the crowd.

You could have heard a pin drop in the audience. People stared in amazement at a sight they had never seen before. Hissing, screaming, gasping for air, this lady's outbursts were beyond belief. At one point the lady even levitated about six inches off the floor. This went on for about ten minutes before she lay completely limp.

I thought to myself, *Oh no, she's dead.*

The silence continued for several more minutes. Then she opened her eyes and stood to her feet. Her countenance had completely changed. Only ten minutes before she looked like walking death, but now she looked completely well.

Wow, I said to myself, *I have just witnessed a living miracle.*

Later that night, the woman told us how severe her medical condition had been. Without intervention, she was going to die. But God! That's all I could say; He is a miracle worker.

This event had left a lasting impact on my mind. I had wondered many times since what thoughts were flooding that lady's mind that night. She knew she was sick and that God was her only option, but I wondered if she knew demons inhabited her body. Regardless, it was the most profound deliverance and healing that I had ever witnessed.

As I continued my drive to church that morning, I remembered another time at World Shakers when God rocked my world. We were hosting our annual conference in a big tent and a similar manifestation of the Holy Spirit occurred, but this time it was for more than one person. I was hosting one of the guest speakers at the conference and she had just concluded her message about God mounting up on the wings of the wind of the Spirit. When she asked me to close the meeting, from the top of the tent fell a miracle anointing that totally engulfed the entire tent. I remembered how it blew in just like the wind she talked about in her message. It was as if time stood still, and we suddenly found ourselves in the eternal presence of God. You could actually feel His tangible presence with your fingertips.

Instead of handing me the microphone to close the service, she slowly returned it to her mouth and declared, "Miracle anointing has just come into the tent. So if you're here and you need a miracle, come forward, and I will lay hands on you."

Hundreds of people flocked to the altar and formed a single line that stretched the entire length of the tent. She began at one end of the line and started praying for people. As she lightly touched each person with her hand, they immediately fell to the ground.

After making her way through about two-thirds of the crowd, she reached out to pray for a woman in the line who loudly blurted out, "I'm not here for myself. I'm here for my loved one who needs a miracle. So if you'll just lay your hands on me, then I'm going to believe that He will touch my loved one and she will be healed."

Immediately, it was as if the miracle anointing was sucked right out of the top of the tent, leaving as suddenly as it came.

The minister prayed for the woman, but when she approached the next person in line, she stopped. Looking at me, she said, "The anointing is gone."

I immediately said to myself, *Yep. It sure is. It went right out the top of the tent.*

"Maybe it has fallen on someone else," the minister said into the microphone.

I shook my head, pointed to the top of the tent and said, "It left."

Then she said, "Maybe if we pray, it will come back."

The moment she said the word "pray," the anointing fell right back into the tent just as it had in the beginning.

"Oh, there it is," she said, and then continued to minister to the rest of those in line. When she finished, the Holy Spirit left because He was done.

The glory of God in that meeting was absolutely amazing. It was life changing and eye opening. I had never known that God operated in that level of power. I had laid hands on the sick before, and I had even cast out demons, but this was power on a whole new scale.

I LEARNED ABOUT THE WAYS OF THE HOLY SPIRIT AND HOW TO OPERATE IN DIFFERENT ANOINTINGS.

As I sat through those two meetings, I remembered asking God, "What do I have to do in order to operate in that kind of power? I want your glory to operate through me that way." God responded by allowing me to witness greater and greater manifestations of His Spirit at World Shakers. World Shakers was a place of power. It was a place of discovery. It was more experiential than theoretical. It was where I learned about the ways of

---

the Holy Spirit and how to operate in different anointings. It completely changed my life.

Interrupting my memories, confusion and anger surfaced. "God, if You were only going to bring me here to rip this ministry away from me, then why did You give me this ministry in the first place? I thought You wanted me to be successful. I thought You wanted to use me for Your glory. Isn't that why You brought me here?"

"I'm moving you. Don't resist." I heard the words as they echoed hollowly in my heart.

I knew God was speaking to me, but in order to explain why He was saying this, we have to start at the beginning.

CHAPTER TWO

HOW IT BEGAN

I have always wanted to do something great for mankind and have felt that my life should count for something more than living and breathing. When I was a child, one of my closest friends was a handicapped girl. Because she had experienced multiple birth defects including hearing loss, she had to wear hearing aids in both ears attached to large battery packs strapped around her chest. The other kids in the neighborhood would often make fun of her and were downright mean to her. Oftentimes I would cry because of what the kids did to her, and I would wish that I could make her normal. Little did I know that God had placed a calling upon my life to help people in the world. I know now that this was a call of God—a call that I would fight for many years.

My experience with God began in 1960. It was a hot summer day in Pasadena, Texas. Our church, Southmore Baptist, was conducting its yearly revival meeting. I was seated beside my brother on the right-hand side of the auditorium midway to the back. I don't recall the message. I wasn't listening to it, but when the altar call was given for salvation, my brother left his seat to go forward.

I remember thinking, *If my brother is going up there for something, then I should probably go too.* So I stepped out from my seat and followed him to the front.

I shook the hand of the preacher, sat down on the front row, and completed a card as instructed by the usher. A box on the card asked the question, "Are you a Christian?"

I looked at the box, turned to my brother and asked him, "Am I a Christian?"

He responded, "Yes."

So I checked the "yes" box on the card.

I stood beside my brother at the front of the church while members walked by and shook my hand and hugged my neck. A week or so later, I was water baptized. This was my earliest remembrance of salvation. I was only eight years old.

My family attended church somewhat faithfully. As a child, I remember going to church with my entire family. In my early teens, I would often attend church with my big brother. Later when my brother left home for college, I attended church on my own. I was pretty faithful to Sunday school, became a part of the youth group, and often sang in the choir. On one occasion, I even spoke from the pulpit in a special youth service. Yet, I had never had a personal encounter with Jesus.

It wasn't until I was nineteen years old and attending junior college that I became aware I needed a personal relationship with Jesus. Back in those days, I was a frequent visitor of the Baptist Student Union. They had the best Ping-Pong table on campus and each Friday they served lunch for all the students. Times were hard, and money was scarce, so I made it a point to go each week for the free meals.

During those meals, I befriended Ron, the BSU director. As I hung out with him, I noticed he had something I didn't have—a personal relationship with Jesus Christ. God started dealing with me about a real relationship with Him.

This went on for a number of months until one morning in freshman history class. The professor was teaching on something about world history, but I couldn't stay focused because of the weight of conviction in my soul. Finally, it got so bad I could no longer sit in my seat. In the middle of the lecture, I stood up, walked out the door, crossed the front lawn of the building, and entered Ron's office.

Before he even had a chance to say hello, I boldly exclaimed, "Ron, I want to get saved, and I want to get saved now."

Shocked, he said, "Well, let's sit down and talk about this."

I replied, "I don't want to talk about it. I don't need to talk about it. I need to get saved right now."

Ron responded, "OK. Let's pray."

**I DROPPED TO THE FLOOR, CONFESSED
AND REPENTED OF MY SIN,
AND ASKED JESUS INTO MY HEART.**

With Ron beside me, I dropped to the floor, confessed and repented of my sin, and asked Jesus into my heart. When

I pulled myself off the floor, I knew I was saved. I had perfect peace.

Later that day, Ron shared the event with a group of his student leaders and wept because God led me to Himself through him. It was the greatest day of my life. I knew victory was mine through the cross. I was a new man.

～∞～

"I KNOW THERE IS MORE OF YOU THAN I HAVE, AND I WANT ALL I CAN HAVE."

This was the very beginning of my walk with the Lord, and it didn't stop there. Three months later, I was driving through the country in my '67 Thunderbird, engaged in conversation with the Lord. I had only been saved a few months, but I already knew there was more to God than I had experienced.

I asked, "Lord, give me more of You. I know there is more of You than I have, and I want all I can have."

As I was praying, God flooded my car with His presence, a tangible presence that caused me to weep for a solid hour. Not understanding this experience, I immediately drove to my church where I found my pastor studying in his office. I shared my experience, asking him to explain what had happened to me. He assumed that I had solely made Jesus the Lord of my life. Yet, walking out of his office that day, I knew something much more than that had occurred. Not until years later did I discover what actually transpired.

In my second year of college, I prepared to go to nursing school and then on to anesthesia school, but I felt a call of God on my life to serve Him in full-time ministry. I was already serving as the music and youth director for a small Baptist church, and unfortunately, this first experience in ministry was less than rewarding. I loved the youth group and enjoyed the music ministry immensely; however, I saw no real future as a minister. A wonderful man, my pastor was a gifted preacher, able leader, and a good friend, but his standard of living disappointed me. He lived in an old and small parsonage, drove a worn car, and his precious wife worked to make ends meet. Knowing this was not the life I desired, I chose to pursue a professional, financially-rewarding career. Thus, I rejected my calling.

By the time I completed my baccalaureate degree in nursing, I had been married for a year and was well on my way to achieving my career goals. After graduation, I took a job with Veterans Administration Medical Center in Dallas. During the first two years, I worked as a staff nurse in cardiac rehabilitation and then in the Coronary Care Unit. In the third year, I landed a position in the medical research department and served with a group of cardiologists who were studying the benefits of aspirin therapy in the prevention of heart attacks. This research later culminated into a universally known fact that the use of aspirin can prevent heart attacks. Even to this day, I feel proud that I was a part of a research team that helped to impact the lives of many people in a positive way.

It was also during this time in my life that my wife and I began attending Beverly Hills Baptist Church in Dallas. Originally a Southern Baptist church, it turned charismatic after Pastor Howard Conatser had a life-changing encounter with the Holy Spirit. You must realize what a big step this was for me. I had heard about charismatic churches as a Southern Baptist, and I was convinced they were in major error. I had no desire to attend one of these churches, but, at the insistence of my mother-in-law, I reluctantly attended a service one Sunday night. I had no idea what to expect but was strangely surprised at my first introduction to the charismatic world. I absolutely fell in love with what I saw. I loved the music, I loved the freedom of the people as they engaged in worship, I loved the message, and I loved the atmosphere of the church. I was so taken by the experience that my wife and I joined the church that very night.

Interesting things began to happen in my life. While attending a new members' class, I heard a teaching about the baptism in the Holy Spirit. The teacher showed us in Scripture how the Holy Spirit was poured out on the Day of Pentecost to the 120 in the Upper Room. They began speaking in tongues as the Spirit gave them utterance and then entered the streets of Jerusalem preaching the Gospel. As the teacher described this experience, I realized what had happened to me that day in the car on the country road. Without knowing it, I had received the baptism of the Holy Spirit.

❦

"IF YOU WANT TO SPEAK IN TONGUES, OPEN YOUR MOUTH AND SPEAK."

Having learned that the baptism of the Holy Spirit was evidenced by speaking in tongues, I realized that I should be able to pray that way. Not knowing how to approach this, I locked myself in the bathroom one day while no one else was home and asked God to give me my prayer language. After waiting awhile for something to happen, I asked God when it was going to come. He replied, "If you want to speak in tongues, open your mouth and speak." I did and miraculously began to pray in tongues. It was a great experience, so great that I continue to speak in tongues to this day.

Even though I received my prayer language, I still did not believe in miracles. One Sunday morning during church, a man jumped out of his seat during the pastor's message and began running and shouting. He ran from one side of the auditorium to the other, turned around, and ran back to his seat shouting all the way. As he took his seat, the pastor continued with his message, and I started to get irritated. I turned to my neighbor and expressed how rude that man was in interrupting the service. The neighbor then informed me that the man had been dying of emphysema only days before and was completely dependent upon oxygen, but that the Lord had miraculously healed him. I was amazed at the testimony but still found it hard to believe. After all, I was a research nurse and knew that miracles did not exist in my line of work.

Only a few weeks later my life was shaken to the core when I was diagnosed with cancer in my throat. The doctor said I had to have surgery right away if I wanted to live. Alarmed at the diagnosis and fearful of the future, when one of the members of my church learned of my condition and asked if I would allow one of the pastors to pray for me, I consented.

I remember thinking, *What do I have to lose? I'm about to die anyway. Prayer may not help, but it sure won't hurt.*

Before Sunday service the next day, I met with Pastor Leavey, a Messianic Jew, to receive prayer for my throat. I have no idea to this day what he prayed because it was all in Hebrew, but when I arrived for surgery the next morning, the doctor was amazed at my condition. He said the cancer had shrunk to the size of a pea and the incision to remove it was no bigger than the width of a Band-Aid. The cancer was completely gone! God had healed my body, and for the first time, I believed in miracles. I was a different man.

GOD HAD HEALED MY BODY, AND FOR THE FIRST TIME, I BELIEVED IN MIRACLES.

Through receiving the baptism in the Holy Spirit and encountering His healing power, God opened my eyes to a brand-new world I didn't know existed. I saw God in a greater way. I discovered that He was a healer, He was a deliverer, and He was a miracle worker. His power was released into my life in a whole new dimension.

Later, I experienced the miraculous power of God again. For years I had struggled with a nicotine addiction and could not kick the habit of smoking. It was a terrible device in my life and a source of major condemnation in my Christian walk. I desperately desired to quit smoking, but had absolutely no willpower to do so. I was hooked. One afternoon while sitting in my living room, I confessed to the Lord that I was addicted.

I said, "God, I'm addicted to smoking and I cannot quit. If I don't quit, I'm going to die. If you don't take this from me, I can never be free. Please take this from me."

In an instant, God removed the desire for smoking from my life. He delivered me, and to this day, I have never desired to smoke again.

In spite of all of these miracles in my life, I continued to run from the call of God. Still pursuing my career, I returned to graduate school and completed my master's degree in nursing. I began writing chapters in nursing textbooks and articles in nursing journals. By the time the aspirin research was completed, I had landed a teaching position at the junior college where I had gotten saved twelve years earlier. Instructing nursing students, once again I felt like I was making a positive contribution in people's lives. I even had the privilege of teaching my own sister who is a registered nurse enjoying a fruitful career today.

During these teaching years, two major things happened that shaped my life. In 1983, I suffered an emotional breakdown triggered by stress related to the demands of my teaching position. By nature I was a perfectionist, and, unfortunately, my lack of teaching experience limited my ability to reach my goals. I endeavored to be the perfect instructor but failed to measure up to my own standards. After trying relentlessly to improve myself, I exhausted all of my emotional energy and spiraled downward toward burnout. One day while I was teaching a clinical session at the hospital, my mind simply stopped. I became disoriented, confused, and didn't even know where I was. I drove myself home, but couldn't even remember the commute.

I walked into the house and informed my wife, "I think I just lost my mind." She looked at me funny, wondering what I was talking about. Not wanting to explain it, I left.

I drove to my mother's house nearby to seek her help. As I tried to explain what happened to me, I realized she didn't understand and wasn't able to help me. Terrified, I pictured myself committed to a mental institution.

I returned home, where my apprehensive wife called one of my former fraternity brothers (yes, I was in a college fraternity) who was a psychiatrist. He saw us the next day for an evaluation. Already prepared to check into the mental hospital, I was relieved when he said, "Larry, you're not crazy. You're exhausted and mentally burned out. Go home, go to bed, and don't get up for two weeks." I took his advice and returned home to bed.

Over the next two weeks, I wanted to die. I was not suicidal, but I wanted God to take my life. I was tired of it. I was tired of trying to be perfect and I was totally exhausted. One day, I asked God to take me to heaven because I didn't want to live anymore.

"God, I want to die. Take me home," I said.

"I'M GOING TO MAKE YOU LIVE AND YOU'RE GOING TO LIVE FOR ME."

At that moment, I heard the audible voice of God for the first time in my life. He said, "Sure you want to die. Anybody can die, but not anybody can live. You're not going to die. You're going to live. I'm going to make you live and you're going to live for Me. Now get up."

Something happened to me when God spoke that. I relate it to the story where Jacob wrestled with the Angel of the Lord (Gen. 32:26-28). As Jacob wrestled, he would not let God go until He removed the curse upon his life.

> And He said, "Let Me go, for the day breaks." But he said, "I will not let You go unless You bless me!" So He said to him, "What is your name?" He said, "Jacob." And He said, "Your name shall no longer be called Jacob, but Israel; for you have struggled with God and with men, and have prevailed."

Because he had been with God, from that day forward Jacob's nature was changed. On the day when God said, "I'm going to make you live, and you're going to live for Me," my nature changed. Something inside me was different. I had been with God. I eventually returned to my teaching position at the college, but I knew I was a different man.

The second event that shaped my life occurred a few months later. Driving home one night with my family following a dinner engagement, we passed my dad sitting in his parked patrol car. He was the city marshal in Kerens where we lived, and it was customary for him to be on patrol most nights. I rode with him on many occasions and loved to spend time with him on the job.

On this particular night, I felt inclined to stop and ride with him as I often did. However, the family was with me so instead, I just honked and waved. Not five minutes later, as I pulled into my driveway and climbed out of my car, I heard a loud crash that sounded like a train colliding with something.

I remember thinking, *That was a strange sound.* Minutes later, my phone rang and a man's voice informed me that my dad had just been involved in a serious collision.

Immediately, I jumped into my car and sped to the scene of the accident. As I arrived, an ambulance was pulling away and a body lay covered on the highway. I walked over to the body to see if it was my dad, only to discover that it was his partner who had just been killed. My dad was the one in the ambulance.

I jumped back in my car and followed the ambulance all the way to the hospital, but by the time I arrived, he was already gone. I never got to say good-bye. That wave was the last time I ever saw him alive. My life was changed forever. My hero was gone.

My dad was a huge part of my life. He never fully acknowledged my salvation experience or my walk with Christ, but I know he was proud of me. A full-blooded Cherokee Indian, he stood six feet tall and was larger than life. Kerens was like the town of Mayberry and my father was Andy Griffith. When people had a need or a problem, they would often turn to him for help. He always extended a helping hand or a good jolt if you needed it. He often portrayed a rough exterior, yet he was very kind-hearted and generous and especially loved children. I loved him very much.

His funeral was one of the largest ones ever attended in Kerens. People came from hundreds of miles away to pay their respects. I can still remember the police honor guard, the twenty-one-gun salute, and the sound of taps playing at his graveside. I'll never forget how the young people in our town were impacted by his death. My dad had touched the lives of so many people. He had done what I had always wanted to do. I was so very proud of him and knew that his life had counted for something. Standing at his grave, I wanted my life to count as well.

STANDING AT HIS GRAVE, I WANTED MY LIFE TO COUNT AS WELL.

Three years later, I finally surrendered to the call of ministry on my life. I was still teaching nursing at the time and working on my doctorate degree in education when I realized that one more degree was not going to fill the emptiness that I felt inside. Once again, I knew there was something more that I needed in my life. I met with my pastor and shared what I felt inside. He immediately discerned the call of God on my life and said, "Larry, God's calling you into ministry." I knew he was right and finally yielded to the Lord.

The date was Sunday, May 25, 1987, the day of our wedding anniversary. My pastor preached a great message that morning, followed by an open altar call where people went forward for prayer. I slipped out of my seat with my wife, and we walked to the front to make a public announcement that I felt called into full-time ministry. I was received by all with open arms, and many told me they had always known my calling was ministry.

I remember feeling such peace in my heart on that day and an assurance from God that I had made the right decision. Little did I know that my journey had just begun.

CHAPTER THREE

GROWING PAINS

The phone rang.

"Larry, I wonder if you would be available to preach on Sunday morning. Our pastor has had a heart attack and we need you. Can you come?" the voice on the other end of the line implored.

I hesitated. It had been nine months since I surrendered to the call of ministry on my life, a decision so exciting that absolutely nothing had happened during that time. Well, I take that back. I did get to preach my first sermon.

While the person on the phone waited, I flashed back. My first sermon was a life-changing event. The pastor approached me about preaching in the main service on a Sunday night, and I was so excited. It was short notice, so I only had a little time to prepare, but I wanted it to be the best. I had absolutely no idea what I was doing, but I acted like I had been preaching the Gospel my entire life. I locked myself away in my office for hours while I pulled out every Bible, concordance, dictionary, and commentary I owned. I chose a very interesting subject for my sermon matter, and I pored over page after page of thesis, exegesis, and reference notes that I found on my subject. My topic for the night was crowns. To

25

this day, I have no idea what inspired to me to preach on this subject, but I know that I preached it with passion.

I arrived that night about thirty minutes before I was scheduled to speak. I was a little nervous and felt butterflies in my stomach, but I had studied and prepared and was as ready as I would ever be. The service started, the singing ended, and then it was my turn to speak. The pastor introduced me, and I stepped up to the pulpit only to look out at an expressionless crowd.

I thought, *Well, here we are. The first step. Destiny, here I come.*

"Would you turn in your Bible tonight to Revelation 4:10 and 11?" I started.

Continuing, I read, "The four and twenty elders fall down before him that sat on the throne, and worship him that liveth for ever and ever, and cast their crowns before the throne, saying, Thou art worthy, O Lord, to receive glory and honour and power: for thou hast created all things, and for thy pleasure they are and were created" (KJV).

OK, I thought to myself, *where do we go next?*

"You see, folks, there are…um…many crowns…um…that we are called to collect in life," I started to say, "and…um…we are supposed to present those crowns to Jesus when we die."

"Now…um…the first crown there is…is the rejoicing crown," I continued. "Now, the rejoicing crown is…um…for rejoicing. Now what you do with that crown is rejoice. So if you feel like rejoicing, you should definitely collect this crown."

I started to sweat. The people weren't amused. I went on, "Now, if you don't feel like rejoicing...um...don't worry. There's another crown called the righteous crown. You earn this crown by being righteous. Now I realize that not all of you in this crowd tonight feel like you have God's righteousness, but that's okay because it's not about God's righteousness; it's about yours."

My mind went blank. What was I saying? Was it God's righteousness that earned the crown or was it our righteousness that earned the crown, or was it righteousness at all? Maybe it was good deeds that earned the crown. Oh no, I couldn't remember what it was!

About this time, I looked down at the front row, and the pastor had his head between his legs, doubled over in pain. I thought to myself, *This is not good.*

I continued, "Now, folks, what you have to understand about crowns is that everyone thinks they need four or five of them, but what I'm here to tell you tonight is that one or two will get the job done. Now if you are the type of person who is very selective about the type of crown you choose, the best one to pick is the glory crown."

I started to think to myself, *God, what is the point of this message?*

I rambled on for another forty-five minutes. By the end of the message, it was clear that the people had no clue what the purpose of the crowns was and if Jesus Himself were standing at the front of the auditorium handing them out for free, they wouldn't want one.

I concluded the message, said amen, and bolted for the side door as quickly as I could. When I was about to escape, the pastor grabbed my arm and pulled me back to the front of the platform. He said, "Now, y'all come on up here and tell Larry what a great job he did." I stood up there as person after person shook my hand and lied right through their teeth as they told me what a great job I had done. It was my most humiliating moment.

That night after the service, my son and I were making nachos in the kitchen. His face wore a very sympathetic look. He had heard the report about dear old dad's sermon and, needless to say, the report wasn't good. Right in the middle of our nacho making, my son looked at me and said, "Well, Dad, at least you've always got a nursing career to fall back on." That said it all. What more was there?

"THE CHURCH NEEDS *MY* BEST, NOT YOURS."

Later that night I went to the Lord and said, "God, if this is what ministry is, I can't do it."

He replied, "Did you do your best?"

I answered, "Lord, I did the best I knew."

He said, "I always want you to remember what your best looks like because your best will never be good enough. From now on, I will begin to show you *My* best. The church needs *My* best, not yours." It was a great lesson learned, a lesson I've never forgotten.

My mind snapped back to the phone call. "Larry, are you there?" the voice demanded.

"Yes," I blurted.

"Are you coming to preach or not?"

"I can make it. When do I need to be there?"

"Sunday," the voice replied.

"Okay, I'll be there," I said, and hung up the phone.

Oak Tree Baptist was a beautiful country church situated in a small one-story white frame building in the middle of the country. The congregation consisted of about a dozen people mostly over the age of sixty, many of whom had been members of the church all their lives. Here I was, a brand-new minister full of passion and zeal, with no clue what I was doing and only my personal church experience to draw upon. Surprisingly, after preaching on Sunday at the church, the people were very impressed with my message. Later, I was asked by the head deacon to stay on as the pastor. He explained to me that the former pastor would not be returning to his duties because his doctor recommended he retire. Sensing the Lord say yes, I accepted the position.

I fondly remember my experience at Oak Tree Baptist. I'll never forget the first wedding I performed there. The bride and groom were a sweet, country couple who decided they wanted to get married right away and asked me to officiate. I had never done one of these before so I figured that preparation was the key to success. I purchased a ministry manual on how to do weddings and followed it step by step. Rehearsal was flawless. The groom stood on one side, the bride on the other, and everyone else knew exactly where to line up. Vows were exchanged and everything went according to plan.

Then the wedding day came and it was time for the real thing. All was going well until I asked for the bride's ring. The best man pulled the ring out and handed it to me. I laid it on the open book I was reading from, and when I got right to the part where I read, "The ring is made of precious metal, a complete circle all the way around," I tilted the book to see the words more clearly. The ring slid out and fell to the floor. I heard a "ping, ping, ping, ping" as the ring bounced off the floor four times and began to roll loudly across the wood floor and down the middle aisle. I watched helplessly as all heads in the congregation turned toward the sound of the runaway ring. My face paled as I looked at the bride and thought, *This woman wants to kill me.* About that time, the bride and groom took one look at each other and started cracking up. I knew I was off the hook.

My time at Oak Tree Baptist was one of the most exciting in my life. For years I had run from the call of God, but there, for the first time, I found myself engaging with my destiny. As a pastor, I fell in love with the people and looked forward to each Sunday in the pulpit. I preached very simple Bible messages on a level that I could express and that the congregation could understand, and I also became very skilled in taking care of people's needs. When someone was sick, I was there. When someone was in crisis, I was there. When someone died, I was there. When someone had a baby, I was there. When the church needed fixing, I was there. The day the window fell out of the building, I was there. Whatever the need was, I was always there.

I WAS THEIR PASTOR AND THE MOST IMPORTANT THING IN THE WORLD WAS MEETING THEIR NEEDS.

I was a shepherd to the people. I was their nurturer, protector, care provider, and chief watchman. Just like Jesus in the Bible, I worked hard to be a good shepherd to my flock. I couldn't stand to see people hurt or upset, and I definitely didn't want anyone to be unhappy in my church. After all, I was their pastor and the most important thing in the world was meeting their needs. Little did I realize that I was embracing a system that would later prove to be very unhealthy.

The church began to grow. God started adding new families and the small work blossomed. People were coming from everywhere. City folks, town folks, country folks—people were flocking to the church. I thought to myself, *Man, this is great. I'm just going to keep taking care of these people, and God is going to keep blessing the work. Life is good.* Of course, with each new family came a new set of needs.

I remember the day I received a phone call from one of my church members telling me her son had just killed his girlfriend. They had been dating for a while and, apparently, had gotten into a heated argument. Tempers had escalated beyond control and before the night was over the girlfriend was dead. I had known this couple for some time, and it came as a great shock to me when I heard the news. Both sides of the family turned to me for help.

I found myself walking a very delicate line between the emotional states of two very devastated families. I remember having to visit the young man in jail in the morning while visiting the other family at the funeral home in the evening. It was a very difficult situation to deal with, but because I was the pastor, it was my responsibility. Each Sunday, one family would sit on one side of the congregation while the other family sat on the other side. I would preach the best sermon I could muster but felt uneasy as I sensed the tension emanating from the families in the room.

Week after week, I found myself asking God, "How does a pastor maintain peace and harmony in an impossible situation like this?"

For months, I struggled with this question. Here I was, the pastor of that church, and my job was to meet all the needs of the people. Yet in this situation, there was no way that I could possibly keep both families happy. I found myself trapped for the first time in a system—a system of impossibilities. I today term this the *pastor system.*

The pastor system is one in which the central focus is meeting all the needs of the sheep. The pastor is a caretaker who works very hard to make certain all the needs of the church family are taken care of. Since the needs of the church family are most important, the family itself is need oriented.

As a result, the family becomes self-centered, self-absorbed, and generally selfish. The mind-set of the body is, *My needs are the most important thing. Pastor, feed me. Change me. Take care of me. It's all up to you.* By design, this system promotes an environment where the church family is dependent upon the pastor for all needs to be met. There is little room for individual development, maturity, or responsibility, except for a small remnant of people who may desire more from the church experience than simply having their needs met.

THE PASTOR SYSTEM IS ONE IN WHICH THE CENTRAL FOCUS IS MEETING ALL THE NEEDS OF THE SHEEP.

The pastor becomes trapped in a system of fulfilling needs. As the needs become so overwhelming that he can't take care of them, he finds it impossible to keep everyone happy. Such was the case at Oak Tree Baptist. I found myself feeling like a failure because two families in the church looked to me as the answer to their pain, yet nothing I could do fixed their situation. It was an impossible task to accomplish, and I was headed for failure.

As time went on, I realized I couldn't meet everyone's needs. I already had two very unhappy families in my church, and on top of that, new spiritual growth created two subgroups of people. The first group I'll call the "planted by the river group." Every Sunday we sang a song that went like this: "I shall not be, I shall not be moved. I shall not be, I shall not be moved. Just like a tree planted by the water, I shall not be moved." Not only did this group of planted people sing with great passion, but they sent me this message every Sunday: "Pastor, you are not going to move me. This is the way I am, this is the way I've always been, and this is the way I'll always be."

The second group of people I'll call the "progressive churchgoers." This group wanted change. They were tired of the old system, they loved the message I preached, and they wanted more of God. I was preaching a message consistent with the charismatic movement and began to move in the power of the Holy Spirit. People were healed and set free in prayer lines, which was a change from the way things had always been done. I even changed the songs we sang and the way we sang them. This progressive group was looking for change and so was I. I felt that God was moving forward, and everyone was supposed to go with Him.

The result of this growth was that I ended up with two very different groups of people with two very distinct sets of needs. This situation completely divided my focus and my energy, and I found myself at the beginning of a church split. As I sought the Lord about how to handle this, I realized that if I continued in this direction, I would do irreparable damage to many people's lives, especially the older people in the church. Because I was a pastor at heart, I could not stand to see anyone hurt, and thus resigned. The response among the congregation was a simultaneous feeling of relief and of disappointment. Yet within myself, I felt an utter sense of failure as I had been unable to meet all of the needs of the church body.

Disillusioned and disappointed, I had no idea what to do next. For the first time, I felt like my friend in the dream who was stuck behind the box truck. I was stuck in a system that wasn't going to change. God had to show me what to do next.

CHAPTER FOUR

AN ANOINTED SETBACK

A week passed and still—no sign of direction. I had no leading from God, and I wondered what He wanted me to do.

God, are you done with me? I thought to myself. *Is Oak Tree Baptist going to be the apex of my success? Please tell me there is something more.*

One Sunday afternoon, I found myself engaged in a prayer meeting with a group of family and friends seeking God for a new leading. Not really knowing what God had planned for me, I was wondering if my ministry life was over.

At this moment, God spoke to me and said, "I want you to plant a new church. This is not going to be like the last church. I am going to do a new thing."

Just like that, I was back in the saddle again. We birthed Highway Fellowship Center and became the first nondenominational charismatic church to ever exist in our town. A fresh dynamic of church life evolved. The chains of religion seemed to fall off people, and God was free to move. People were saved, healed, delivered, filled with the Holy Spirit, and experienced freedom in their lives. The services were glorious. People lifted their voices in praise and worship and danced as they sang. Women played tambourines and men clapped their hands. People came forward every Sunday for prayer, and the anointing was so strong that many would fall to the floor under the power of God.

During this time, I was critical of television evangelists. I watched them each week and criticized their methods. I wasn't sure if they were inspired by the Holy Spirit or just by their own idea. Then one night, I had a dream. In this dream, I saw our church worship leader as she led during worship time. I distinctly noted the dress she wore, the style of her hair, the earrings in her ears, and the shoes on her feet. God told me in the dream to go over and blow on her like the television evangelists did, and that when I did, He would release the power of His peace. Then the dream ended.

The very next service, I was amazed when the worship leader walked in the door and was wearing the exact outfit I had seen in my dream. I thought to myself, *God, You are up to something.* The service was underway, and we were right in the middle of a song when the Holy Spirit prompted me to go up to her and do what I saw in the dream. Nervously, I stepped out of my seat and onto the stage to blow on her as God had directed, but when I got there I didn't have the courage to do it.

I stood there a little longer and heard the Lord say, "Blow on her," but I still didn't move.

Three times He told me to do it before I realized I'd better blow on somebody, or God was going to let me have it.

About that time, the song ended, and I announced to the congregation that tonight the Lord was going to release the power of His peace. I closed my eyes to pray, expecting to blow on the worship leader as instructed, but at the end of my prayer I opened my eyes only to find a tall man standing in front of me. He had come to the altar for prayer, and, not knowing what to do, I took in a breath and softly blew on him. Nothing happened.

I thought, *Lord, I look like a complete idiot.*

The Lord replied, "Well, if you're going to blow, then *blow.*"

So with all I could muster, I took the deepest breath I had ever taken, and I blew as hard and as long and as loud as I possibly could. When the breath finally left my lungs, I heard a sound like a mighty oak tree snapping in two and falling to the ground. To my amazement, I looked up and the man had fallen to the floor.

I thought to myself, *Dear Lord, what have I done?*

I then turned to the worship leader and softly blew on her. Just like God told me in my dream, He released the power of His peace, and she wilted to the floor like a spaghetti noodle. Immediately, everyone in the room bolted to the altar to experience the same thing. I started down the line, blowing on each person, and as I did, they fell one by one. The peace of God overwhelmed each one of them, and the atmosphere of the sanctuary was filled with His tangible presence.

We had many more services like that. Highway Fellowship Center was a progressive church. In my opinion, we were cutting edge. We had the best music, the best people, the best preaching, the best anointing, and the best ministry of any church around. During this time, I truly felt like I was doing something great for God. Lives were transformed, and God used me powerfully, yet I continued to facilitate the pastor system.

THE NEW MIND-SET BECAME, "WHAT CAN THE ANOINTING DO FOR ME?"

What kept the pastor system alive in this new church was my ignorance of my role. The people in my church were very unique with unique needs, and once again, I felt it was my job to take care of them. The difference, though, was that I was now depending on the power of the Holy Spirit to meet those needs instead of trying to meet those needs myself. The people were being changed and impacted by the power of God, but the new mind-set became, "What can the anointing do for me?"

I thought I was building a church where God could do what He wanted to, but in actuality, I was building a system fueled by junkies who were only interested in God if He could give them their Holy Ghost fix each week. Once they couldn't get their fix, they bolted down the street to the next church that could give them what they needed. And once again, it fell on me as the pastor to meet those needs—this time through the anointing.

One of the dysfunctions of the pastor system is that it creates a cycle whereby Christians bounce from church to church looking for the "ultimate experience" that is going to fix all of their problems. They become *self*-absorbed in the music, or the preaching, or the programs until they can find something that is going to meet their needs. The problem, though, is once they discover that the current program doesn't meet their needs, they run out the door looking for another program that will. This creates an endless cycle of church hopping and dissatisfied saints who can never find their place and function in the body of Christ.

The other rotten fruit of the pastor system is lack of true growth. Because the system is family oriented and "me centered," all growth is turned inward. The anointing in the senior pastor draws people to the congregation, but the truth is that most of these people come from other churches. With problems or circumstances they want changed, the pastor's gift is what they are seeking. Growth does occur in this system, but since it usually occurs from recycled sheep seeking something more, it is not true church growth. Contented pastors assume the church is growing, without realizing the growth is stimulating a dysfunctional system.

As Highway Fellowship Center continued to grow, a greater demand pulled upon my anointing, and I realized that if I was going to continue in this type of ministry, I needed more training. I began to pray for the Lord to show me where I should go. For months, I felt like I was not meeting the needs of the people, and if I could only go to Bible school, I would have the training necessary to meet all these needs. I knew I was still stuck on the freeway behind the box truck, but at least now I was trying to move over.

This was an interesting time in my life. I began to search for the best Bible school in the country that I could attend. I would select one and ask the Lord, "How about this one?"

He would answer, "This one's good, but it's not the best." So I would instantly reject that school because I needed the best.

Some months later, I was attending a minister's conference when I picked up a brochure for World Shakers Bible College in California. It was then that the Lord spoke to me and said, "This one is best." Immediately, I knew what was next: I turned my blinker on and started shifting lanes. I was headed for California.

CHAPTER FIVE

BOOT CAMP

For mile after mile, the open road never seemed to end—first Amarillo, then Albuquerque, then Flagstaff, then Barstow, and finally California. I had arrived! On my way there, the Lord spoke these words to me: "Launch out into the deep." I didn't know what God was talking about, but He began to talk to me about Simon Peter in Luke 5.

> So it was, as the multitude pressed about Him to hear the word of God, that He stood by the Lake of Gennesaret, and saw two boats standing by the lake; but the fishermen had gone from them and were washing their nets. Then He got into one of the boats, which was Simon's, and asked him to put out a little from the land. And He sat down and taught the multitudes from the boat. When He had stopped speaking, He said to Simon, "Launch out into the deep and let down your nets for a catch." But Simon answered and said to Him, "Master, we have toiled all night and caught nothing; nevertheless at Your word I will let down the net." And when they had done this, they caught a great number of fish, and their net was breaking. So they signaled to their partners in the other boat to come and help them. And they came and filled both the boats, so that they began to sink. When Simon

Peter saw it, he fell down at Jesus' knees, saying, "Depart from me, for I am a sinful man, O Lord!" For he and all who were with him were astonished at the catch of fish which they had taken; and so also were James and John, the sons of Zebedee, who were partners with Simon. And Jesus said to Simon, "Do not be afraid. From now on you will catch men." So when they had brought their boats to land, they forsook all and followed Him. (Luke 5:1-11)

I can so identify with Peter in this story. Here he was just minding his own business when, one day, Jesus came to him and turned his world upside down.

"Launch out into the deep," the Master said.

Peter must have been thinking, *Yeah, right. Who is this man? What does He know about fishing? I've been fishing my entire life and could do better in one night than He could do in a day.*

Yet something in Peter took this man at His word, and he felt compelled to respond to the message. He launched out into the deep. To his great surprise, he not only caught a load of fish, but a glimpse of his eternal destiny as well.

Much the same, when God told me to launch into the deep, He was showing me that He had marked my life for His purpose and was preparing me for something that I had never experienced before. I started to realize that to experience what I'd never had before, I had to do something I'd never done before. Selling my house, leaving my church, packing up the moving van, and driving 1,400 miles across country to a land I had never been was a complete walk of faith. If I didn't know at the time that World Shakers was God's best, I would never have made the move.

"Launch out into the deep." These words resonated within my heart once again.

God, I thought, *this is either faith or I'm the biggest fool who has ever lived.*

Bible school started in August with over 150 students who had gathered from the United States and around the world. Excitement was in the air, and I was alive with anticipation. Finally, I was going to be trained in the proper way to build a church. I was going to learn how to build the best pastor system in the world and finally figure out how to take care of everyone's needs. Speakers from all over the world came to teach us. They taught on subjects like prayer, authority of the believer, Old and New Testament, gifts of the Holy Spirit, spiritual warfare, how to build a strong inner man, and the lives of God's great men and women.

Each morning, the dean of the Bible school would start our day with an hour of prayer. This wasn't just any kind of prayer. We were taught to pray out of our inner man as we were led by the Holy Spirit. Most students would pray in tongues while the dean led in both tongues and English. The atmosphere of the room was electrified and oftentimes sounded like a roar or deep rumble. Each morning I loved to be a part of prayer. I felt like God was building things inside of me that had never been built before. It was as if God was forming a new spiritual DNA. Old mind-sets were changing, and God was opening a whole new world of life in the Spirit to me.

During this time, I learned about life in the Spirit. I learned that God created man as a three-part being—body, soul, and spirit. Most of us live out of our body and soul, but never build up our spirit. It is our spirit that relates directly to God, and it is the primary way we communicate with Him. If we want to learn how to communicate more effectively, we have to build up this part of our being. Paul said it like this in Ephesians 3:16, "That he would grant you, according to the riches of his glory, to be strengthened with might by his Spirit in the inner man" (KJV).

It is the Holy Spirit who renews our minds with the truth of the Word and transforms us into the image and likeness of Christ. He is the person of the Godhead who reveals to us the mysteries of the Father. He is the one who strengthens our spiritual man and gives us the ability to pray in the Spirit with power.

The more I got to know the Holy Spirit at World Shakers the more effective I became at flowing in His power. I learned how to build an effective prayer life and move things in the Spirit through prayer. Many times I would stand in intercession for people, situations, nations, and circumstances and see God move in profound ways.

World Shakers was more like a boot camp than a Bible school. Students weren't scholars; they were trained to be soldiers. The emphasis of the school had little to do with academia. The leadership could care less if you learned in which book of the Bible "Daniel and the lion's den" could be found. They wanted to know if you could cast out a demon. Could you shake a nation? Could you tear down a stronghold? Could you preach with power? Could you do great works for God? That is what mattered most.

World Shakers was my first introduction to a paradigm that was different than the pastor system. The philosophy was one that emphasized discipline, self-sacrifice, regimented thinking, and fulfilling destiny in the face of adversity. You learned that your flesh and your soul are your enemies, and your spirit man is your only friend. To be successful in this environment, you had to learn to kill your flesh and silence your emotions so that your spirit man could dominate your being. Living out of your flesh was not an option. Only the spiritually strong survived.

In this Bible school, you would always hear terms like, "Gird it up. Press in. Pull it down. Tap into the spirit. Kill your flesh. Subdue your soul. Invade the nations. Take the city. Tear down the strongholds. You are God's army, God's best, God's chosen recruits, and are called to take the nations for Him." This gospel was pumped into our heads night and day. As a matter of fact, we so believed the message that we became quite militant about it. Our attitude was to either accomplish God's mission or die trying.

The goal of the Bible school was to graduate and send out as many students onto the mission field as possible because the vision of the leader was to establish mission bases in every country of the world. He trained his students to storm the nations of the world and take them by force. They were taught to preach the Gospel with power, without apology, without reservation, and in the style he prescribed until all in the world had heard the gospel—his gospel. It took many years to fully understand what this system was all about, but after being in it for a long time, I came to call this the *training system*.

This system was so different than the pastor system I was used to. In the pastor system, the main focus was on your flesh and your soul and how to get all of your needs met. In stark contrast, the training system was just the opposite. Needs were not important. What *was* important was sacrificing yourself for the sake of the greater cause.

IN A TRAINING SYSTEM, THE FOLLOWERS ARE EXPECTED TO CONFORM TO THE LEADER'S STANDARDS.

In a training system, the followers are taught the message of the leader. They are expected to conform to the leader's standards. They are trained to be just like him, so they can measure up to his expectations and carry out the vision of his ministry. The perceived merit of submitting yourself to this system is that you will have the opportunity to share in the anointing of the leader. An intense atmosphere of competition and dominance is created as those closest to the leader position themselves to receive the greatest portion of his anointing.

Affirmation and approval in this system are received from the leader only as he deems appropriate for each follower. Usually this affirmation comes from the leader when he feels that the follower has measured up to his standard and shows himself to be loyal to the vision. A trainee who does not hold to the leader's expectations will undoubtedly have a sense of failure because he is not able to measure up. What makes this system even more challenging is that the leader's standard can change at any moment, only intensifying the frustrations of the followers.

World Shakers created an environment in which relationships with one another took a backseat to the vision of the leader. There was little nurturing, and love was an ugly four-letter word. As a matter of fact, love was the weakest word in the dictionary. When someone would have a personal problem or needed help, the response of the leadership was to get over it. Move on. Toughen up. Press into God. Don't be weak.

Weakness was considered our enemy. Weakness did not impress God. What God was impressed with was our strength. God wanted us to be strong—strong in power, strong in might, strong in our inner man, strong in our authority. Weakness was not tolerated. We were trained to be overcomers.

I was so amazed at the level of sacrifice and selflessness that students exhibited to be a part of this school. I watched as my classmates denied their needs, pushed down their emotions, and laid their lives down for the sake of the call. I knew of students who even slept in their cars because they didn't have a place to live. I remember one student who would shower in public restrooms, at the beach, or any public place because all of his money had to go toward tuition. I knew another student who would rollerblade to school because she couldn't afford other transportation. I knew of students who couldn't afford to eat and would fast for days upon end. I never in my life saw such an environment where people literally sacrificed their lives.

I would often ask myself, *Why are these people doing this? What's in it for them?* Obviously nothing. It was all for the sake of the call.

One of the problems with the training system is that it can open the door for potential abuse by the leader. Unless the leader has true accountability from a genuine father in the faith, this system can engender a dysfunctional environment whereby the people become subject to every whim of the leader. Once the system becomes dysfunctional, there is no way of escape without the intervention of the Holy Spirit.

UNLESS THE LEADER HAS TRUE ACCOUNT- ABILITY FROM A GENUINE FATHER IN THE FAITH, THIS SYSTEM CAN ENGENDER A DYSFUNCTIONAL ENVIRONMENT.

Of course, during these days I didn't see all of this. I thought this system was normal. I thought I had gotten around the box truck. I was shifting—shifting fast into the other lane and heading out on the highway. It wasn't until years later that I discovered where I went wrong.

CHAPTER SIX

THE SECOND MAN

I was nearing completion of my first year of Bible school and wondering again what was next. Would I head back to Texas? Would I take up the pastorate? Would I go onto the mission field? I started seeking God for an answer and didn't have to wait for long. At this time, the founder of World Shakers, Pastor John, approached me about launching his new church. He had a vision for a local church that would be known for its ability to govern and influence nations, and he wanted me to join his staff as the associate pastor.

I prayed about his offer, reminding the Lord that my goal in attending Bible school was to learn how to build a church. I told the Lord that I still wasn't sure how to do it. While I learned many things in school, I cannot say that building a church was one of them. He responded by saying that the best way to learn how to build one was to help Pastor John build his. So I took that as a confirmation and accepted the position.

For the next seven years I would mature in my role as the second man. I learned that this was one of the most critical positions in a church, a position that could make or break a ministry. My service to Pastor John was unto the Lord—he may have hired me, but it was God who had appointed me. I purposed in my heart daily that I would be faithful, trust-worthy, loyal, and effective in my duties to help build the church.

World Shakers Christian Center was much like the Bible school in the sense that it mainly focused on the vision of Pastor John. Everything revolved around him. He was very charismatic, an excellent communicator, and extremely anointed in the pulpit. He was known in many circles for his keen prophetic gift and ability to speak the direct word of the Lord into a situation.

I learned many things from Pastor John. He was my mentor. Because I was the second man, I was as close to him as few ever got. I was able to see his good side, his bad side, and his ugly side. I witnessed his life and his lifestyle first-hand.

Pastor John was very faithful to prayer. He had spent years in prayer and in the spirit learning how to hear the voice of the Lord. He had an incredible ability to discern people and situations very accurately. I never knew a man like him who could so easily access the throne room of God.

I remember asking him one day, "Pastor John, how long does it take you to get into the presence of God?"

Without hesitation, he looked at me, and his counte-nance changed instantly as he accessed heaven. Immediately, I felt the presence of God enter the room. After a few seconds in the eternal, he snapped back to earth and said, "About that long." I was absolutely amazed. The entire atmosphere had been saturated with the presence of God in only a few seconds.

It was Pastor John who taught me how to pray. His manner of prayer was unlike any that I had ever known before or since. He was a man of great faith, and his prayers reflected his faith. When he prayed, something always happened. He would call things into being that did not exist. He would move obstacles out of the way and bring into manifestation God's power. He would release the word of the Lord through prayer, and situations would change. He would lay hands on people, and demons would come out. He was truly a man who was led by the Spirit of God.

Another thing I learned from Pastor John was how to cast out demons. I discovered that demons come in different forms and work in all kinds of people. Pastor John would almost always hold prayer lines at the end of his message and pray for people who were oppressed by the devil. He would operate in great power as he took authority over the demons and commanded them to leave. I saw all kinds of manifestations when he would pray. Some people would convulse, some would scream, some would writhe on the floor, some would become combative, some would curse, some would scream accusations, and some would even run. But generally, all of them would be delivered. Pastor John walked in a tremendous deliverance anointing.

One time when I was helping Pastor John pray for the sick in a prayer line, I was praying for a lady when, suddenly, a hand touched my back and a surge of power went through my body and into my hands. Immediately, the woman I was praying for fell to the ground under that power. I turned around to see that it was Pastor John who had laid his hand on me. That is the kind of power he walked in.

Pastor John spent most of his time on the road traveling. Rarely a week went by that he was not in another state or country preaching somewhere. Because he traveled so much, my main responsibility was to oversee the church and cover the pulpit while he was gone. I spent a great deal of my time preparing sermons and developing ministries within the church. I helped create the children's ministry, youth ministry, music ministry, outreach ministry, small group ministry, and the church leadership team.

I TAUGHT THE PEOPLE THAT THE PURPOSE FOR THEIR LIVES WAS TO GIVE THEMSELVES TO THE VISION OF THE LEADER AS UNTO THE LORD AND SERVE IN THE MINISTRY.

Because we were a training system, I mainly operated by the philosophy and methodology of my leader. I taught the people that the purpose for their lives was to give themselves to the vision of the leader as unto the Lord and serve in the ministry. Ultimately, their purpose was to serve the needs of the church. If the church needed an outreach team, they were it. If the church needed altar ministers, they were it. If the church needed small group leaders, they were it. If the church needed money, they were it. If the church needed missionaries, they were it.

I remember one year when Pastor John told the people that if they wanted to remain a member of the church they were required to go on at least one mission trip. He said that the calling upon the church was to go into the entire world and preach the Gospel, and if they didn't go, they obviously did not hold to the tenets of the faith. As a matter of fact, I had to go on a mission trip, too. It was my very first one. Little did I know, this was the beginning of Pastor John's vision to send hundreds of his church members and Bible school students as missionaries into every nation of the world to extend his ministry.

Worship at World Shakers was unlike any I had ever heard. We rarely sang slow songs because we did not have the concept of intimacy with the Father and being before His throne. Instead, we focused solely on high praise. Our philosophy was that high praise broke down the strongholds of the enemy and released our spirit man to gain spiritual ground for God. We were taught to be strong in our praise. We shouted, we yelled, we bounced up and down and pointed our finger in the air, and sang choruses over and over proclaiming, "God is a warrior" and "He is a man of war."

Our times of praise were accompanied by outbursts of strong tongues and warfare prayer. We felt that Satan was an enemy who was at our heels at all times and who had to be pushed back. Satan was always after us. He was after our kids, after our health, after our money, after our destiny, and after our very lives. We had to enforce God's authority against him at all times. If you weren't praying warfare prayer, you were losing spiritual ground.

Life in the spirit was an uphill battle that was never won. It didn't matter how much you prayed or how much you battled against the enemy, he was always a constant threat. We lived in a constant state of war; we never had peace in our minds, peace in our hearts, or peace in our lives. We didn't know that the battle was already won by Jesus Christ on the cross; we thought it was up to us to win the battle against Satan every day.

Pastor John was recognized as one of the forerunners of the warfare message in the body of Christ. The message was based on Ephesians 6:12,18: "For we wrestle not against flesh and blood, but against principalities, against powers, against the rulers of the darkness of this world, against spiritual wickedness in high places. Praying always with all prayer and supplication in the Spirit, and watching thereunto with all perseverance and supplication for all saints" (KJV). He preached that Satan was someone who had to be defeated and that we as Christians had to pray fervently to overcome him. Because this was the main message that formed the foundation of our church, we were acutely astute in the art of warfare. No one knew better than we how to pray offensively against the schemes of the devil. When it came to a face-off, the devil didn't have a chance.

This atmosphere of constant warfare produced an environment where people were paranoid and suspicious of anything that looked or felt like a devil. If you walked into our church and sneezed the wrong way, five people would come over to you and cast the sneezing spirit off of you. If you even looked at someone in the wrong way, they would turn to their neighbor and say, "I wonder how many they're packing," meaning, "I wonder how many demons they have."

Because we were a warlike people, the concept of God's love was never conveyed to the congregation. I likened our environment to some of the warlike cultures that existed in ancient times. Warriors were honored and respected based upon their merits in battle, but that was all their lives counted for. If they weren't fierce warriors, they really didn't have any value. To be someone, you had to learn to fight. It was the same way at World Shakers. Value was given based on performance. Those who performed well were rewarded with affirmation and promotion, but those who didn't were viewed as weaklings. It was an extremely unhealthy environment that was destined for destruction.

The fact that this environment was unhealthy was really not apparent to me in the early years of the church. I just thought it was the way that a megachurch was supposed to operate. It wasn't until my family became affected by this environment that I started to see the destructive nature of the training system.

CHAPTER SEVEN

A HOUSE DIVIDED

When I responded to my calling to become the associate pastor at World Shakers, my life was not the only one affected by my decision. It was a family decision as well. My wife Kathy had also attended Bible school at World Shakers at the same time I did and graduated alongside me. When I later took the position as associate pastor, it was understood that Pastor John was hiring not only me but my wife as well. We were considered a husband-and-wife team and served in the ministry together.

Kathy presented some real challenges to Pastor John and the ministry at World Shakers. By nature, she is a mover and a shaker, and anything she's around that isn't glued down usually gets shaken up. She's always been like this. From the first time I saw her in high school, what I loved most about her was her ability to see the truth in every situation. Throughout our marriage, her gift of discernment has saved us from many wrong decisions that I would have made otherwise.

Kathy's leadership at World Shakers proved to be quite a challenge to the system. Because she walked in such a high level of discernment, she was often viewed as a threat, especially when it came to matters regarding our family. Many times Pastor John would come to me and say, "Larry, you have got to get your wife under control. She is a problem to the ministry." I would then respond with, "Well, what's the problem?" But he could never give me a straight answer.

This went on month after month, year after year. The more it did, the more I sensed a threat to my marriage. I started feeling like Pastor John actually wanted me to get a divorce and would have been happy if I had done so. This bothered me greatly, so one day I confronted him about it. I told him I felt he was interfering with my marriage and to stop it. He told me I was a liar, and although he vehemently denied my accusation, I did not believe him.

The next event only solidified my belief that Pastor John was indeed opposed to my marriage. On the very special occasion of our twenty-fifth wedding anniversary, Kathy and I planned to renew our vows before the church. We asked Pastor John to officiate for us; however, he declined. To make matters worse, he refused to even attend the ceremony. The church was packed with members who were excited to share in our special moment, but Pastor John never showed up. I ended up having to do the event myself with the assistance of my son Brandon. It turned out great, but I was disturbed that the man I had served for seven years wouldn't even come to my ceremony.

Shortly after that, my wife and I embarked on a cruise to the Caribbean to celebrate our wedding anniversary. A week later, we returned on a day that just so happened to coincide with our midweek church service. We barely had enough time to get home and unpack before we had to get ready for church. My wife decided to stay home that night to unpack while I went on to service. I was standing next to Pastor John during worship service when, for no reason at all, he hit me backhand across the chest and growled, "Where is your wife? Why isn't she here?" Completely shocked, I simply told him she was at home. He was obviously angry for some reason, but never told me why. Later, he apologized with no explanation. I never fully understood what happened that night, but I knew that something had significantly changed in our ministry relationship.

As time went on, Pastor John and I became more distant. I didn't know why he was irritated with me, until one day, it finally dawned on me where the problem lay. Pastor John was threatened by my wife because she would not conform to the system he had created. She was a nonconformist, an independent thinker, and lived outside the box. Pastor John could not control her, manipulate her, or make her do what he wanted, and it bothered him. It was then I realized I had to make a choice. I had to either divorce my wife and marry the system or divorce the system and stay married to my wife. My loyalties were divided, and I was being challenged by the system. That's when I began praying, "God, if this system is not going to change, please move me."

The training system went beyond my wife; it also affected my children. From the very beginning, my son Matthew decided that he was not going to be part of it. He had a very strong discernment gift much like his mother, and he was able to spot deception from a mile away. In the first year of the church, Matthew told me that there was something desperately wrong with Pastor John and the system. He said, "Dad, if you don't get away from here I'm afraid of what might become of you and your ministry." Because he was only thirteen years old at the time, I disregarded his words and felt that he was being rebellious. In response, he decided that he would do the only thing he knew, which was to scream for my attention; he turned to sin as a means to cope with the situation. This only strained our relationship and made it impossible for us to get along.

By the time Matthew was fifteen, our relationship was so damaged that he left home. Kathy and I were devastated. Seeking Pastor John's advice, I asked him what to do. His response was to disown him. Perplexed, I thought to myself, *How does one disown his own son? I can't.* At this point, I realized how much I had neglected my family for the sake of the system. All of the teaching about forsaking all for the sake of the call meant nothing to me at this point. I had lost everything there was to lose. I had lost my own son, and it would be many years before I would get him back.

***

I REALIZED HOW MUCH I HAD NEGLECTED MY FAMILY FOR THE SAKE OF THE SYSTEM.

The final straw came with my other son Brandon. Brandon had grown up as a teenager at World Shakers. He was an outstanding member of the youth group, a passionate Christian, and a fiery preacher. His walk with the Lord really began when he discovered his calling for full-time ministry at age fifteen. Desiring to pursue a future in ministry, he decided to go through Bible school at World Shakers and upon graduating went onto the mission field. Out of all the members in my family, Brandon was the most indoctrinated with the philosophy of the training system and how it worked. He was the perfect soldier, always doing what he was told, never questioning authority, and idolized Pastor John in every form of the word. Pastor John was his hero to the point that he became his clone. In my opinion, this is what set him up for disaster.

It wasn't too long after Brandon arrived on the mission field that he began having problems. He told me the problems started after he preached one of his fiery sermons at a local church and assaulted some of the principalities in the area. The fallout from the message was incredible. It was as if he had dived into Satan's lair and attempted to fight him and his cohorts one on one (like he was taught in Bible school), but the enemy easily overpowered him. For months afterwards, Brandon came under serious spiritual attack and didn't know what to do. His mind became tormented by the devil, fear gripped his heart, and panic set over his entire body. He would hallucinate at night, feel demons in his room, black out at times, and would even forget who he was. Later he would tell me that he couldn't even remember his childhood, where he was from, or why he was there. In short, he was having a mental breakdown brought on by an onslaught of hell against his life.

As a father I did the only thing I knew to do. I went to my spiritual authority (Pastor John) and told him, "We have to help this boy. He is falling apart."

I was completely flabbergasted by his response. He said, "Larry, I sent that boy over there on purpose. I knew it was the hardest country in the world to be a missionary in, and I sent him over there to get the crap knocked out of him. If he were my son, I'd let him die over there."

I could not believe what I had just heard. Not only had this man tried to break up my marriage, but he had now assaulted both of my children. Finally, I realized that the environment I was in was completely destroying my family, and, for the sake of saving their lives, I had to make a decision quickly.

Soon after, as I was shaving in the bathroom before Sunday service, I heard the words, "I'm moving you. Don't resist." I knew it was God. He had heard my prayer, and He was moving me. I knew from this moment on that the system was not going to change, and I had to leave.

Right about this time, Pastor John decided to call me into his office one day. He said, "Larry, you're tired. You need a break. I want you to take thirty days off. I want you and your wife to go anywhere in the world you want to go and I'll pay for it. The only request I have is that you not call the office or call home or think about ministry or the church while you are gone."

At the time, I thought that Pastor John saw that I was under great stress in my life and that he was sending me on this vacation to give me a rest. It wasn't until I returned home from my trip that I realized his purpose for sending me away. The day I arrived home, I found a note stating that I needed to call Pastor John before returning to the office because he had made some changes.

I tried calling him multiple times, but he avoided my phone calls for a week. Finally one day he called me into his office and said, "Larry, I have taken the church back."

I responded with, "How can you take something back that's always been yours?" There was no response.

Then I asked, "What would you like for me to do?"

He said, "I don't know. I guess go back to your office and just counsel people."

I remember going back to my office after that meeting wondering, *How is this all going to come down? God, you said you were moving me, so I guess this is it.*

Later that afternoon, my wife and I were both called into a meeting, and my wife was told that while she was gone on vacation, the office had been more peaceful than it had ever been. Things happened like clockwork when she was gone, but when she was there things were disastrous. Obviously, she must have a devil because the problem was with her.

The following day, Pastor John called me back into his office and asked me what I was going to do about my wife.

Amused at the question, I jokingly responded, "Well, I've thought about that. I think I'm going to keep her."

Pastor John was not impressed and started staring me down. I then said, "I'll tell you what. Let's just cut to the chase. It is obvious that you want me out of here. I'll make it easy for you. I resign."

Pastor John immediately reeled back from his desk and retorted, "I don't receive that."

I responded with, "It's not open for discussion. I'll have my resignation on your desk this afternoon." I walked out of his office for the last time. It was finally over. A week later, my wife and I were on our way back to Texas.

CHAPTER EIGHT

DONE WITH MINISTRY

It was our second day on the road. We were driving through Arizona on Interstate 10 when, without warning, the road in front of me disappeared. In its place I saw a huge movie screen and a series of events that were about to take place. I was the main character in the movie, and in the first scene, I saw myself buying a house. In the second scene, I saw myself getting a job. In the third scene, I saw myself packing up our condominium in California. In the fourth scene, I saw the moving truck driving down the interstate, and in the fifth scene, I saw myself going to a church. While I watched these scenes, the Lord spoke, "You will settle north of Dallas, and there I will establish you." Then at the end of the last scene, He spoke again saying, "When you get to this part, you will begin to pray and, as you pray, I will unfold your next season." The movie screen finally vanished, at which time I realized that I had just had an open vision.

God had to speak dramatically to me at this point in my life. As far as I was concerned, I was done with ministry and never wanted anything to do with it ever again. I was burned out with the pastor system and betrayed by the training system. Since these were the only two systems I knew, I figured there was nothing else ministry could offer me, and I wanted nothing to do with either system. Yet, it was obvious that God was not done with me.

In the months following, everything that God showed me in the vision came to pass in the exact order in which He revealed it. When the last part of the vision was completed, I knew I was to begin to pray as the Lord instructed.

At this time, I began to gather with two couples whom I trusted very much. They knew what I had just been through with the church in California and had my very best interests at heart. We began to meet weekly in an apartment in Dallas on the campus of Christ for the Nations to pray.

"YOU SPENT THE LAST SEVEN YEARS OF YOUR LIFE BUILDING A MAN'S MINISTRY. NOW YOU WILL SPEND THE REST OF YOUR DAYS BUILDING *MY* KINGDOM."

During one of these nights in prayer, God once again showed me an open vision. In this vision, I saw a large building that was brownish in color with a stone facade. As I stood in the parking lot gazing at the building, I realized that the Lord was standing next to me. As He stood there, I gazed up at the building again and saw illuminated letters that read Kingdom Life Christian Center.

The Lord immediately spoke to me, "You spent the last seven years of your life building a man's ministry. Now you will spend the rest of your days building *My* kingdom." At this moment, I realized this would become my life's assignment.

The Lord then took me into the building and gave me a tour. We walked down a long hallway with doors on each side. He opened the doors one by one, and in each of the rooms something different was going on. In one room, I saw praise and worship and glory filling the room. In another room, I saw children being taught and nurtured. In another room, I saw ministers being trained and equipped, and it was obvious they were being prepared to engage in their life assignments. In another room, I saw missionaries packing their bags preparing to go to the mission field. In another room, I saw outreach occurring and people were being ministered to. In another room, I saw a court in session and an innocent person on trial, but it was as if he were being judged righteously and God was protecting him. There were also other closed doors that He did not open.

After visiting the last room, the Lord turned to me and said, "In My Father's house are many rooms." I immediately knew that each room the Lord had just shown me represented a dynamic of my new assignment and that the closed doors represented other dynamics that would be revealed in time. We walked out of the building, and the vision ended. *Build the kingdom?* I thought to myself. *What is the kingdom?*

I had no clue what this meant. I had spent my whole ministry life building churches. After all, wasn't that the reason I went to California in the first place? I went there to learn how to build a church, and that's exactly what I did. I learned about programs, building plans, moving and shaking people, and getting a man's vision built, but I was never taught how to build the kingdom of God. As a matter of fact, I never recall the word "kingdom" mentioned once.

After the vision, I realized I needed to find someone who knew more about the kingdom than I did. I later shared the vision about Kingdom Life with the prayer team at Christ for the Nations, and that was when one of the team members asked me if I had ever heard of Apostle Jim Hodges. She told me that he had pioneered the kingdom message and lived right there in the city of Dallas. Figuring this man must know more about the kingdom than I did, I knew I had to meet him.

Within a week, my wife and I were sitting down together at a meal with Apostle Jim. We shared our story with him—what we had been through, what we had experienced, and what we felt our new assignment was. Amazingly, he responded with open arms, and I felt like I had met a true father in the faith. Isn't it incredible how God knows exactly who we need and how to connect us at the right moment?

After meeting Apostle Jim, I started to dive into the Bible to find out about the kingdom of God. First, I had to learn what the kingdom was. The Hebrew word for kingdom is *malkuth* which is translated "reign, realm, or royal power." It is described in Psalms as something that is glorious, everlasting, righteous, and over all other realms. The concept of kingdom was first mentioned in the Bible in Genesis 1:28: "Then God blessed them, and God said to them, 'Be fruitful and multiply; fill the earth and subdue it; have dominion over the fish of the sea, over the birds of the air, and over every living thing that moves on the earth.'"

In this account, we see God as the heavenly King over His entire creation, commissioning Adam to reign as His representative on earth. As an appointed earthly king, Adam was given the job of ruling over the garden. He had God's full authority to exercise complete dominion in the garden as long as he submitted to God's instructions. It is clear that God's original plan was for mankind to serve as His appointed earthly kings for the purpose of establishing and ruling over the earth realm.

In Exodus 15:18, we see another example of the kingdom when Moses states, "The Lord shall reign forever and ever." The word "reign" is the Hebrew word *malakh* which is translated "be king" or "exercise the functions of a monarch." In essence, what Moses declared was that the Lord shall be King and exercise the functions of His monarchy forever and ever. This declaration came just after God (as King) had conquered Pharaoh (an earthly heathen king), thereby releasing His nation of kings (Israel). It is clear that Moses had a revelation of God as King over all the earth.

In the New Testament, the Greek word for kingdom is *basiliea* which is translated, "royalty, rule, realm, and reign." It is first mentioned in Matthew 3:2 in the preaching of John the Baptist who heralded, "Repent, for the kingdom of heaven is at hand." While John was heralding this cutting-edge message of the day, Jesus came to him to be baptized. When He did, John immediately recognized that the King of glory had shown up and that God's kingdom had come with Him.

Jesus' earthly ministry was completely focused on preaching the message of the kingdom. In Matthew 4:23, we see Jesus going about all of Galilee, teaching and preaching the Gospel of the kingdom and healing all who were sick. The most significant thing about Jesus' message is that signs and wonders always followed, validating the truths about the kingdom.

Look at some examples of the kingdom in Jesus' teachings. In the Beatitudes, He tells us the poor in spirit are blessed because theirs is the kingdom of heaven. He adds, the persecuted are blessed because theirs is the kingdom of heaven. As He teaches about the Law of Moses, He tells us that unless our righteousness exceeds that of the scribes and the Pharisees, we will not be able to enter the kingdom of heaven. In the model prayer, He teaches us to pray for His kingdom to come and His will to be done in earth as it is in heaven. In the same prayer, He says that the kingdom belongs to God and the power is His forever. He declared one day to the Pharisees that if He casts out devils by the Spirit of God, then the kingdom of God has come. His teachings, His parables, and His miracles all had one purpose—to demonstrate the kingdom of God. Even after His death and resurrection, Acts 1:3 states that Jesus spent forty days speaking to the apostles about the kingdom of God.

The kingdom goes even beyond Jesus' teachings. The book of Acts records the apostles preaching the message of the kingdom. In Acts 14, we see Paul and Barnabas strengthening the disciples of Lystra, Iconium, and Antioch, exhorting them to continue in the faith and, through many tribulations, enter the kingdom of God. In Acts 19, Paul is in Ephesus speaking boldly in the synagogue for three months, reasoning with and persuading the Jews concerning the things of the kingdom of God. In Acts 20, Paul is bound in the Spirit for Jerusalem, as he recounts his ministry journeys to the elders at Ephesus, proclaiming how he had preached the kingdom of God. Finally, the book ends with Paul in Rome preaching the kingdom of God and teaching the things which concerned the Lord Jesus Christ (Acts 28:31).

I LEARNED ABOUT A SYSTEM WHERE GOD IS THE SUPREME BEING OVER ALL, AND THAT HIS LAWS GOVERN ALL THINGS ABSOLUTELY IN HEAVEN AND ON EARTH, INCLUDING THE AFFAIRS OF MEN.

As I studied this subject in the Bible, I began to see that the theme of the kingdom was woven into the very fabric of every chapter. I could see a God who was interested in establishing His system of government over the entire earth realm. I learned about a system where God is the Supreme Being over all, and that His laws govern all things absolutely in heaven and on earth, including the affairs of men. I began to call this the *kingdom system.*

The best example I could find of this system in Scripture was in the Old Testament where God established Himself as Supreme Ruler over Israel. Because of His covenant with Abraham, God chose Israel as a nation that would bear His name and exercise His authority. He chose them as His representatives upon the earth to establish His rule and reign. God was their leader. He was their Cloud by Day, He was their Fire by Night, He was the Lord of Hosts, He was their Rear Guard, He was their Fortress, He was their High Tower, He trained their hands for war, He caused them to triumph over their enemies, and ultimately, He was their King.

The reason this system worked for Israel was because God was exalted in His proper place in the hearts of His chosen people. They knew who He was, and they knew who they were. Things worked perfectly. Enemies were defeated, cities were taken, evil kings were dethroned, and God was made King over every place they put their feet. It wasn't until Israel decided they were going to do things their own way that everything began to fall apart; when, in essence, they disengaged from God's system and set up their own kingdom. Destined to fail, it wasn't too much later before Israel was completely dismantled and scattered as a nation. They had traded God's system for a system of their own.

Later, God restored His system. Even though Israel lost sight of God's kingdom plan, He redeemed it through Jesus Christ. When Jesus came to earth, one thing that characterized His ministry was that He only did what He saw His Father doing. When He would heal a sick person, it was because He saw His Father healing that sick person. When He cast out a demon, it was because He saw His Father casting out the demon. Jesus said in John 14:10, "Do you not believe that I am in the Father, and the Father in Me? The words that I speak to you I do not speak on My own authority; but the Father who dwells in Me does the works."

⚜

SICKNESS, DISEASE, OPPRESSION, AND EVEN DEATH OPPOSE THE KINGDOM OF GOD.

So the question presents itself, "Why did the Father want to heal sick people and cast out demons?" The main reason is that sickness, disease, oppression, and even death oppose the kingdom of God. The Bible says in Romans 14:17 that "the kingdom of God is… righteousness and peace and joy in the Holy Spirit." So it is evident that these works of darkness oppose the operation of God's Spirit in the earth. When confronted by the authority of God's kingship, the kingdom of darkness has to flee from the kingdom of God every time.

God wants to show His kingdom through the life of Jesus. He wants the world to know that He is still alive and well and on His throne. He still has a plan for mankind and His plan involves ruling His created world. Satan has done a great job in blinding the minds of people to this truth, but through the demonstration and power of God's own Son, He has opened the world's eyes to the fact that He is still King of kings.

This concept fascinated me. The more I read about the kingdom, the more I wanted to know. I became very aware that what I had preached for the past fourteen years had very little to do with the kingdom of God. It had more to do with systems of man than systems of God. I had spent all those years operating in a pastor and training system, but I had never been a part of a kingdom system. I then began to wonder, "Where does church fit in all of this?"

I had to study more about the kingdom to understand the answer to this. As I did, I discovered the church and the kingdom were not the same thing. While the kingdom of God describes the rule, reign, and realm of God, the church describes the people of God. In the New Testament, the Greek word for church is *ecclesia* which means "the community of believers." The church is made up of born-again believers who have been given access to the kingdom of God through the atoning work of Christ. Paul said it like this in Colossians 1:13, "He has delivered us from the power of darkness and conveyed us into the kingdom of the Son of His love."

As the redeemed church, believers are given full rights of sonship through Jesus Christ. Through growth and development in their relationship with God, they mature in their understanding of spiritual sonship and increasingly transform their mind-sets into the image of Jesus Himself. Personal character and human nature are continually changing into His likeness; and righteousness, peace, and joy in the Holy Spirit become hallmarks of the kingdom of God operating within them. They become a heavenly minded people who live on the earth, governed by the desires of their heavenly Father rather than their own. Therefore, the church is the expression of the kingdom of God on the earth while the kingdom itself is the display of God's power and authority over every created thing.

THE PASTOR AND TRAINING SYSTEMS TEND TO BECOME KINGDOMS OF THEIR OWN.

The kingdom of God is bigger than the church. The Bible says in Psalm 24:1 that "The earth is the Lord's, and all its fullness, the world and those who dwell therein." God's kingdom not only encompasses the church, it extends to the whole world—every person, every creature, every creation, and every thing that has ever existed. The church may be the expression of the kingdom, but it certainly is not the kingdom itself nor is it to become a kingdom unto itself.

The main problem I noticed while ministering in the pastor and training systems is that these systems tend to become kingdoms of their own. Many times they begin with a focus on God or a desire to know Him, but end up becoming dead, lifeless, man-controlled systems that fulfill selfish desires.

I was finally shifting into a new revelation. For the first time, I definitely felt like I was getting around the box truck and building something that was going to truly honor God and get the job done. I knew that a new church plant was in my immediate future, but I determined that if I was going to be a part of building another church, I would only build one that mirrored the original design. God was going to have to show me how to build a kingdom church.

CHAPTER NINE

STARTING OVER

A man once paraphrased Psalm 127:1 by saying, "The best-laid plans of man will fail unless God crowns them for success."

It had been seven months since God had shown me the picture of Kingdom Life in the vision. Still uncertain about what a kingdom church should look like, I continued to pursue Apostle Jim for additional insight and revelation. Our ministry relationship started to grow closer, and I finally decided that it was time to join his apostolic network and become fully ordained through the Federation of Ministers and Churches International. I did so in May 2001.

It is interesting to note that Apostle Jim was a successor to my former pastor, Howard Conatser, of Beverly Hills Baptist Church where I was introduced to the charismatic movement so many years before. Beverly Hills eventually became Church of the King and was pastored by Apostle Jim for many years. He also taught for ten years at Christ for the Nations in Dallas, Texas, where he pioneered the message on the kingdom of God.

Early on, the Lord made it very evident to me that Apostle Jim was to be the spiritual father of our work. Given my years of ministry experience, I knew how critical it was to have a spiritual covering. For so long, I had seen in the body of Christ a major difference between covenantal relationship and being connected in name only when it came to spiritual covering. By this I mean, I wasn't looking to be credentialed by a ministry on paper only; I was looking for a personal relationship with someone who would be a true spiritual father. This person had to be one who would love me as a son and have my best interests at heart. I knew that Apostle Jim was this kind of man. After sharing my plan for starting Kingdom Life, he gave his blessing and we began.

The day was November 4, 2001. Our first service was held on a Saturday night in a dirty, dingy day school because it was the only facility we could find for a church service. Facilities where churches could meet were in short supply in our city, so we actually had to share the building with a Lutheran church. Because the Lutheran church had already secured the facility for Sunday morning services, we decided to meet on Saturday nights.

Shortly after I signed the contract with the day school, I received a phone call from the Lutheran pastor. "Hi there, I'm Pastor Brad. I pastor the Lutheran church that meets on Sunday morning. I heard that we are going to share the building together, and I was just wondering where you are going to park your trailer."

I responded with, "I don't have a trailer."

Pastor Brad then asked, "Well then, where do you plan to store your equipment?"

I replied, "I don't have any equipment."

To my surprise he said, "That's great!"

"It is?" I asked.

"Yeah. Why don't we partner? You can use my trailer and our equipment. You set the church up on Saturday, and I'll tear it down on Sunday."

I thought to myself, "Partner? I didn't even know partnerships existed among churches." I'd been a pastor for fourteen years, and I had never heard of this, much less done it. What a concept—my first experience in working with a kingdom-minded church.

We started having services and things were going great, except that I felt like I was building the same old thing. Fact is, old habits die hard and mind-sets don't change in a day. Even though God had instructed me to build the kingdom, I mainly was still operating under the old pastor and training systems. True, I was learning about the kingdom concept, but I had no idea how to implement it.

The first step in changing from a pastor and training system to a kingdom system was to begin preaching what I had recently learned about the kingdom. I had to let the kingdom concept begin to change my thinking; it had to be more than just Bible knowledge or personal study. It had to become my way of life, so it could change the lives of others.

To help me shift, God began to show me that whenever He builds a thing, He first constructs it by revelation. For instance, Noah was told to build an ark that would save the human race even though he had never heard of such a thing, much less built one. A boat was an entirely new concept to him. It had never been done before. Yet in God's heart there was a need for a boat to be built, and He looked to Noah to accomplish it. Even though God gave him the building plans and the time and means to accomplish the project, Noah had to see it clearly before it could be done. The same was true with me as I tried to build the kingdom system. I had to see what a kingdom system looked like and experience it first-hand. I knew that if I was going to build correctly, I would need progressive revelation.

THE CHURCH IS NOT A BUILDING, BUT RATHER THE PEOPLE OF GOD IN THE BUILDING.

As I remained faithful to implement the vision God had shown me, I began to discover the dynamics of a kingdom system. One of the first things I learned about a kingdom system is that the church is not a building, but rather the people of God in the building. I remember the day that revelation came. I was preaching to the congregation one Sunday morning when a thought popped into my head about going to church. I told the people, "When asked what church you go to, your response should be, 'I am the church.'" That became such a revelation to me after I spoke it. After years of preaching in pastor and training systems, it had become apparent to me that most Christians base their identity and value on where they go to church. They take great pride in being a member of a certain church and when asked where they go to church, they proudly answer, "I go to First Baptist" or "I'm a World Shaker." Without realizing it, they are trading their identity in Christ for their identity in a church organization and replacing a kingdom mind-set with a church mind-set. For the first time, I began to see this very clearly.

The next revelation I received about the kingdom system is that it focuses more on living outside the four walls of the building than on the inside. I began to see that the typical church structure today is designed as an inward model to draw as many people as possible into the building. The church spends countless hours and thousands of dollars in outreach programs, marketing strategies, published material, special conferences, and media to attract and integrate people into its facility. The church thinks it's accomplishing its goal by winning people to Christ and reaching as many people as possible, but the problem with this model is that it has created a church environment in America that is impacting nothing but itself. We are nothing more than a system of recycled sheep who think that because our church is growing in size we must be doing something right for God. Our success is based on numbers, programs, and what can be done to keep the people happy, when in reality, building the kingdom of God has little, if nothing at all, to do with these things.

THE KINGDOM SYSTEM FOCUSES MORE ON LIVING OUTSIDE THE FOUR WALLS OF THE BUILDING THAN ON THE INSIDE.

The focus of the kingdom system is getting people outside the four walls of the building to demonstrate the kingship of Christ in their everyday lives. As the church, we may gather for worship, teaching, training, and fellowship, but the ultimate goal is to take Jesus to the streets. Outreach does not focus on increasing the local church size or converting people to our system; outreach focuses on extending the influence of God's kingdom into culture.

A KINGDOM SYSTEM FOCUSES ON CHANGING CULTURE.

A kingdom system focuses on changing culture. It has no desire to try and get the world into the church; its goal is to get the church into the world. Because the world belongs to King Jesus, kingdom people feel that the world is where they should live their lives and demonstrate their faith. They realize that the kingdom cannot be built in an internal manner behind church walls; it has to be built in society as it is demonstrated by those who believe. Believers are not called to hide in plush buildings or behind stained glass windows. They are commanded to herald the message of Christ the King in society. The church, as it is today, has done a terrible job in building this concept into Christians and has failed to change culture accordingly. The typical church feels that Adam and Eve surrendered the world to Satan and his devices, and that the only hope for mankind is to get as many people saved as possible before abandoning earth on the way up to heaven. Afterward, they think that God will judge the world for its sin, but they will all be safe with Him.

Kingdom people have a different revelation. They believe that God still owns the world. He created it, and it was

His design. He made it perfect in His image and He has no plans of abandoning it. Even though Satan took advantage of man in the garden and sin entered the world, God still had a plan to redeem the earth for Himself. Jesus came not only to restore man back to relationship with God, but also to set into motion God's plan to bring the world back into its original design. As it was in the beginning when Adam ruled in the garden, so it will be in the end when the church will rule the earth. This is one of the main emphases of the kingdom philosophy.

AS IT WAS IN THE BEGINNING WHEN ADAM RULED IN THE GARDEN, SO IT WILL BE IN THE END WHEN THE CHURCH WILL RULE THE EARTH.

The next thing about the kingdom system is that all generations are important to God. God always has generations in mind when He builds something. For example, Abraham's call was not only for his own family, but for all future generations. Jesus came not only to save the lost of His day, but to preserve future generations for His Father's kingdom. Each new move of God will always provide for future generations. Kingdom people will always build so others can take up where they leave off and grow stronger, deeper, and attain higher levels of kingdom accomplishment.

We can learn something from earthly kings that can be applied to the kingdom system. A wise king will raise a son or daughter to succeed the throne and carry on his dynasty long after his death. He will invest himself in that successor, imparting his knowledge, wisdom, and anointing to make certain that the kingdom will continue to grow after he is gone. The successor will often share the scepter with the king while he is alive and will then receive it when passed down from the king himself. This insures that the old will be invested into the new and yet make room for the new to have its full expression in the kingdom.

ALL GENERATIONS ARE IMPORTANT TO GOD.

Luke 5:37 illustrates this succession. In this parable, Jesus teaches that new wine is poured into renewed wineskins and both are preserved. The new wine of future generations converges with the wine of current generations, and the strength of both are preserved going forward. The old generation blesses the new, and the new generation carries on with a strong foundation and a model to give out to future generations. In the kingdom, room is made for future generations by investing heavily in their lives. Years and years of countless hours and prayers are invested in each successor, so they can carry on long after the older generation is gone. The successor then repeats the cycle with his/her successor to propagate the system. Thus, all will flourish in God's sustained presence, and generations to come will continue to grow and advance in the purposes of God.

Revelation of the kingdom now poured in at an increasing rate. I didn't completely understand everything God was doing yet, but the people in the church were catching on, and we were starting to accelerate around the box truck. Finally, we were disengaging from the pastor and training systems.

CHAPTER TEN

LOVE IS THE GLUE

It was the year for day schools and day cares. It had been three months since we started Kingdom Life, and we were looking for a Sunday-morning venue. By mistake one day, a letter arrived in the mail announcing that another local church in the community was vacating their current meeting location. I called the pastor of the church to verify, and he told me that the letter had been written to members of his church only, and I must have gotten one by mistake. How many of you know that God doesn't make mistakes?

I immediately contacted the facility where they were currently meeting on Sunday mornings and asked if it was available. Would you believe it was? Would you also believe that it was a day care? Like I said, it must have been the year for day schools and day cares. The owner informed me that the facility was available, and we immediately signed a contract to move in.

The move, although welcomed, presented a big challenge for us. In order to use the facility we had to purchase our own equipment and a trailer to store it in. Not only did we not have any equipment, we also didn't have the money to buy it. Back in that old place again, I sought the Lord for direction. In response, He simply said to go get what I needed.

Obediently, I purchased a trailer, a complete sound system, and fifty folding chairs. I spent thousands of dollars that the church did not have at the time. Would you believe that within the following week two checks arrived that completely covered the cost of the equipment? The amazing thing—we had said nothing to anyone about any of this. God had provided in a supernatural way, and once again we knew we were right where He wanted us to be.

WE HAD TO LEARN THAT UNCONDITIONAL LOVE MEANT WE LOVED PEOPLE REGARDLESS OF WHAT THEY COULD OFFER US.

One of the hardest things for me to work through during this phase of building Kingdom Life was learning how to relate to people differently than I had before. In the pastor system, I had learned to relate to people by always being there to take care of their needs. In the training system, I had learned to relate to people by connecting them to the vision of the leader and making them feel like they were fulfilling their destiny. To be quite honest with you, in the kingdom system I really didn't know *how* to relate to people. To make matters worse, many of those who attended the church in the early years were actually victims of the pastor and training systems. Most weeks it felt like the blind leading the blind, but somehow I knew we all had to shift if we were going to build the work properly.

To help us make the transition at this point, we each had to gain an understanding of God's unconditional love. We had to learn that, instead of relating to people by what they could do for us or what we could do for them, we had to learn that unconditional love meant we loved people regardless of what they could offer us. It was a whirlwind revelation; soon relationships all around me began to change.

The first relationship that needed changing was the one with my son Matthew. A healing process had to take place, one that actually began prior to leaving California when God confronted me about my lack of love for him. I was praying for him one day when the Lord said to me, "You don't love your son."

I replied, "What do you mean I don't love my son. Of course I love my son."

God said, "No, you don't. You love yourself. You love your ministry and your success, but you don't love your son. If you want to save your son, love him."

I knew God was right. I truly *didn't* love my son, and I didn't know how. Matthew was a nonconformist. He refused to conform to the training system that I was a part of and was resistant to all I stood for. Because of this, I was disappointed in him. Yet, what I didn't realize was that in my disappointment of his behavior, I had rejected him as a person. I truly *didn't* love my son, and I remember praying, "God, I don't know how to love my son. You must show me how."

Over the next few years, God showed me how to love him. The first thing I did was stop judging him for his behavior and start accepting him as a person. While I still did not condone his lifestyle, I purposed in my heart that I would love him unconditionally. Secondly, I began to communicate with him every day. Not a day would go by that we did not speak. If I didn't see him in person, I would call him on the phone. By doing this, I began to engage in his life and take an interest in whatever he was doing. I would constantly encourage him and purposed to be there for him any time, any place, and in any situation.

One of my greatest joys was conducting his wedding ceremony. He was getting married to Liane, a beautiful and gifted young Christian woman whom I knew from World Shakers, and I really wanted to perform his wedding ceremony. I remember calling him to say, "Matt, I would never presume a thing, but I want you to know that if you would like for me to perform your wedding ceremony, I would be very honored to do so." To my delight, he told me that would be great and he would love for me to. I was thrilled beyond measure.

OUR RELATIONSHIP WAS BEING HEALED. FOR ME, THIS WAS THE KINGDOM IN ACTION.

Matthew and Liane had a beautiful ceremony. It took place on a scenic bluff overlooking the Pacific Ocean on a lovely day in May. I specifically remember sharing what the Lord told me to speak that day. I told them that marriage would have its ups and downs, but love would be the glue that would hold them together. I then concluded the ceremony unlike any wedding I had ever done before. I requested both sides of the family to come forward to pray a prayer of blessing over them. Standing there, I still recall the sense of

God's unconditional love being released in prayer over my son and new daughter. I knew at this point that our relationship was being healed. For me, this was the kingdom in action.

Our relationship continued to be restored and God started doing miraculous things in Matt's life. Five years later, I received a phone call. It was Matthew. He said, "Dad, I've got some good news. The greatest thing happened to me today. I gave my heart to the Lord, and I wanted you to hear it from me." There were no words. I dropped the phone and began to cry. The love of God had restored my son, and it was love that ultimately drew him to the cross. Today, Matthew is a changed man. He is a passionate Christian who loves God and His kingdom with all his heart.

The next person to get a revelation of God's unconditional love was my son Brandon. As you recall, he experienced a terrible time on the mission field. He came home after six months of intense trauma only to go into a deep, dark depression for almost a year. He felt like a complete failure because he was not able to accomplish the mission for which he had been trained his entire life. He had failed to measure up to the standard of the training system, and because he is such a perfectionist, he truly felt that his life was over.

One particular night, Kathy and I were attending a church service when Kathy felt a spirit of death come over her while the minister was preaching. She grabbed my hand and said, "Larry, please pray for me. I feel like I'm dying." We began to pray softly so as to not draw attention to ourselves, and, for what seemed like an eternity, we faced a spirit of death head-on until it left.

Kathy and I came home from church later that night and saw Brandon's Bible open on the desk. She knew something was up because he had not opened his Bible since the day he came home from the mission field. It wasn't until the next day that she found out what had happened.

Brandon tells the story like this. During the evening while we were at church, he was sitting in bed watching television. He said that he felt an evil spirit climb up in the bed next to him and the spirit started speaking in his ear, "Brandon, this is the night. Go ahead and kill yourself. You have no reason left to live. You are a failure. You will never be anything. You will never recover from this. You will never move on. Tonight's the night. Do it."

Brandon owned a gun and felt tempted to pull the trigger that night, but he became so afraid that he ran outside and dumped his shotgun shells in the garbage. He tells the story that after he came back into the house, the Spirit of God came over him, and he started to pray. He had not prayed since the day he left the mission field, but on this night, the overwhelming grace and mercy of God covered him in his moment of need. He says that he wrestled with the spirit of suicide in prayer for about fifteen minutes, and then just like that, the evil spirit left the house never to return.

Immediately, the presence of God filled the house, and God began to speak to him. He told him to turn to Psalm 121 and spoke to him the words, "The Lord is your keeper; the Lord is the shade at your right hand. The sun shall not strike you by day, nor the moon by night. The Lord shall preserve you from all evil; He shall preserve your soul. The Lord shall preserve your going out and your coming in from this time forth, and even forevermore."

God then played a video for Brandon of his time on the mission field and showed him exactly what happened. He showed him how the enemy came in like a flood and that Brandon was not able to resist him. He even showed him how the devil had asked for his life to take him off the earth, but how God had intervened and told the devil that he couldn't have him. God showed him that He loved him so much that even when Satan himself had come for his life, God said, "No." In essence, what He was saying to Brandon was that he was too valuable and too important to be given over to the devil, and, no matter what, He would never give him up. This revelation changed Brandon's life. For the first time, he felt the unconditional love of God. It forever changed his perception of God, and it was the biggest turning point in his life. God went on to restore his mind, deliver him from the depression, and put him back on the road to his destiny. My son is a success story. Today he is a husband, father, minister, and businessman. He is sold out completely to the Lord.

WE REALIZED THAT WE NEEDED ONE ANOTHER AND THAT GOD NEEDED ALL OF US WORKING TOGETHER TO FULFILL HIS PURPOSES ON EARTH.

By learning about the concept of unconditional love, God made it possible for all of us to relate to people in the kingdom. We stopped looking at them as numbers on the roll, people in the seats, and money in the bank and started looking at them as God's creation, fearfully and wonderfully made. We began to see that their purpose and destiny was not to build the leader's vision, but to expand God's kingdom in the earth. They were valuable, not because of what they could do, but because of who they were in Christ.

It had now become clear that as a kingdom system, the body was not to be comprised of independent visionaries but rather interdependent family members. Simply stated, we realized that we needed one another and that God needed all of us working together to fulfill His purposes on earth. Yet, even though we work together for the common cause of the kingdom, we still retain our uniqueness as individuals with gifts, callings, and anointings that are critical for the whole church. God places a demand upon the church that we be corporate minded and rooted and grounded in His love, but at the same time we can still fulfill our individual destinies.

The love of God is the most powerful force in the universe. It holds all things together and keeps all things connected in God's righteous way. It is the only way to build the kingdom. Though challenges with people and circumstances try to deter us from building on the foundation of God's love, it's always the heart of the Father that keeps us on track. Loving God and each other is how we shift from low gear to high gear when accelerating around the box truck.

CHAPTER ELEVEN

THE KINGDOM MODEL

"This building is simply too small," Kathy said.

"I couldn't agree more," I replied.

It had almost been four years since we moved into the day-care facility. It had seemed so large the first day we met there, but the walls had now closed in and we needed a new place to meet. An elementary school was available only a mile away and had four times the amount of space. So we moved in and started building the next phase of Kingdom Life.

It was during this phase that God greatly began to unfold the plan for a kingdom church model. When Kingdom Life was being birthed, God gave me a five-year blueprint showing how to structure the church, how it would grow, and how it would mature. He said I would be amazed when I saw what He would do in five years and the first five years were indeed amazing! People's lives were changed, kingdom revelation poured forth, and we felt like we were pulling ahead of the box truck; however, five years was coming to a close, and once again, I needed new direction.

During this time, God said, "The first five years are coming to an end. Now you will begin to evolve into the full expression of what I have called and destined you to be." After He spoke these words, the Holy Spirit began to unfold a whole new picture of what a kingdom church looks like. The picture is much like that in Ezekiel 1:16 where the prophet describes the wheels within a wheel.

In this picture, I saw wheels of circles within circles, each one representing a dynamic operation of the kingdom church. Each circle was interconnected to the others, and collectively, they operated as a single wheel in complete fluid motion, like a tire that travels down a highway.

A KINGDOM PEOPLE WILL ALWAYS EMBRACE THE HEART OF JESUS AS THEIR ULTIMATE SOURCE OF EXISTENCE BECAUSE THEY CANNOT FUNCTION OTHERWISE.

The center wheel or "hub" represents the King of glory. It expresses the core revelation that Jesus is King. The King is the essence and substance of the kingdom. He reigns sovereignly and supremely in absolute power and authority. A kingdom people will always embrace the heart of Jesus as their ultimate source of existence because they cannot function otherwise. A scriptural example of a kingdom person like this was the apostle John. John was a man who was captivated by the heart of Jesus, a man whom he loved with all of his being. He would lay his head upon the bosom of Jesus and could hear the very air moving through His lungs as His heart beat. He knew that the heart of the King was the doorway to His kingdom, and that without embracing this revelation, the kingdom couldn't be built.

Jesus further exemplified this revelation in His earthly ministry. He came into the earth realm for one purpose—to fulfill His Father's heart. His mission was not only to seek and to save the lost but also to destroy the works of the devil, to return forfeited authority to the church, and to pave the way for the church to reestablish His Father's dominion over the earth. Jesus was totally captured by His Father's heart as we must be. Like the apostle John, we must be connected to God's heart. We must know Him as the Lion and the Lamb, the Alpha and the Omega, the Savior and the King who is seated at the right hand of God and who will return to earth when all the enemies of the kingdom are "under His feet" (1 Cor. 15:25). We must know that His kingship, His kingdom, and His church have no end.

The heart of the King will always be toward establishing the kingdom of God. Jesus prayed, *"Thy* kingdom come, *Thy* will be done in earth, as it is in heaven" (Matt. 6:10 KJV, emphasis mine). John the Baptist said it like this, "He must *increase*, but I must *decrease*" (John 3:30 KJV, emphasis mine). Isaiah prophesied, "For unto us a child is born, unto us a son is given: and the government shall be upon his shoulder: and his name shall be called Wonderful, Counsellor, The mighty God, The everlasting Father, The Prince of Peace. Of the increase of his government and peace there shall be no end, upon the throne of David, and upon his kingdom, to order it, and to establish it with judgment and with justice from henceforth even for ever. The zeal of the Lord of hosts will perform this" (Isa. 9:6-7 KJV). The revelation here is that the *King* is the reigning, ruling monarch to whom all honor, worship, and devotion is to be given.

A church without the King at its center will never be a true expression of the kingdom of God. Church systems today may save the lost, minister to the sick, cast out devils, and engage in noble and worthy ministries, but if they cannot connect with the King, they will never fulfill the ultimate desire of God for establishing His kingdom-rule over the earth. This is one of the great tragedies of the church. Jesus even echoes this in Matthew 7:21-23 when He says that not all who profess His name and engage in the works of the ministry will enter His Father's kingdom. Only those who know Him intimately in covenant relationship will be granted access. Knowing him as King establishes a solid foundation that will ensure success and glory for the kingdom of God (Matt. 7:24).

There can be no kingdom without a king and no king without a kingdom. The greatest expression of the kingdom of God is the church, the family of God. It is the second wheel in the picture God showed me and forms a circle around the center wheel, the King of glory. The family is comprised of those who have met Jesus, are born again, and have entered the kingdom of God (Col. 1:13). When this happens, there is an instantaneous change of citizenship (Eph. 2:19). This change is described as an adoption by the Father into His family. This family then lives in covenant relationship with the King, is subject to His laws and code of conduct, and enjoys the privileges of covenant relationship.

Family has always been a part of God's operation in the earth; family is foundational to the kingdom of God. In the beginning of time, the Trinity was a family of three who were in covenant relationship and operated as one. When the Trinity created the earth, God saw that it needed a human who would be likened to Himself, and thus, created Adam in His own image and likeness. He then saw that Adam needed his own family, so He created Eve and set in place the family system. The two became as one even as the Father, Son, and Holy Spirit were one in heaven. God further exemplified the value He placed on the family system when he later destroyed the human race in the Great Flood, but decided to spare not only Noah but his entire family. By sparing the family, He made a statement that family is His foundational institution on the earth and is worth preserving.

The family of God (the Trinity as well as the church) is fueled by the love of the Father. It is a covenantal love that serves as the foundation stone upon which all relationships within the family grow and flourish in a healthy way. As family, relationships develop with one another in three ways: first, from the overflow of intimacy with the King; second, with a fathering spirit from the elders and leaders; and third, with a commitment to embrace one another and grow in grace and love.

A HALLMARK OF THE KINGDOM CHURCH IS THE FUNCTION OF SPIRITUAL PARENTING.

A hallmark of the kingdom church is the function of spiritual parenting. In the family, the grandparents and parents in the faith connect with the sons and daughters by the Holy Spirit and form relationships which are held together through covenant bonds of love, peace, and honor. A dynamic flow of interrelationships evolve which foster healthy growth and development, protection and security, corporate identity, and stability among family members. While formal training and teaching is necessary, it is the wisdom, knowledge, and blessing of the spiritual parents that truly cause the sons and daughters to mature.

Like all congregations of believers, kingdom people have needs that require attention. However, personal needs never become the primary driving force of the system. Needs will occur, but as the church family emerges in spiritual strength and understanding, they will provide support in times of need. As this happens, crises are handled and challenges are met by the church family. This produces a mind-set that church is not all about "me" or getting "my needs met;" instead, church is about functioning in my role as a believer and assisting others with their needs.

Because family is foundational in the kingdom system, the role of the pastor dramatically changes in this system. Rather than taking sole responsibility to meet all the needs, the pastor engages church family members to minister to one another as needs arise. He also identifies, trains, and releases those within the family who can shepherd or directly care for the needs of the body. As these shepherds build and establish relationships within the family, pastoral support becomes a way of life rather than a work of the ministry. Each family member develops a deep love and value for the other person and engages in loving, nurturing support without being directed by the pastor to do so. Love compels everyone to reach out to their fellow family member to encourage, strengthen, and help him or her overcome in situations that arise.

The third wheel I saw in the picture had the word "army" written upon it. The Lord spoke to me and said, "While the kingdom of God is first a family, it is also an army." These two dynamics are forever woven into the spiritual DNA of the kingdom system. In order to advance and fulfill the Father's heart within culture, the family must be trained as an army to become ready to engage the enemies of the kingdom.

An example of this can be found in Genesis 14. In this chapter Abram has a family crisis. His nephew Lot is taken captive and all of his goods are stolen by an enemy king. Word reaches Abram of the situation, and he rallies his household together to save him. Genesis 14:14 states, "When Abram heard that his relative had been taken captive, he called out the 318 trained men born in his household and went in pursuit as far as Dan" (NIV). This passage clearly shows us that Abram's family was *also* a trained army. When the need arose to fight for Lot, the household of Abram knew how to engage the enemy. In the same way, the church must not only be strong and loving, she must also be a trained army.

A true family will fight side by side preferring the other over self. Remember the band of brothers in the 101st Airborne Division in World War II? They were an army infantry division renowned for their valor during the Normandy Invasion and the Battle of the Bulge. History so eloquently shows them fighting side by side, loving one another, looking after one another, preferring each other over self, and engaging the enemy with fierceness and courage. Their very lives were dependent upon strength born out of relationship. They never abandoned one another in the face of danger or overwhelming odds. Bound not only by honor and duty, family ties knitted them together as one. The adversity they shared made them brothers. In the same way, it is love of family members for each other that causes them to become a powerful army.

Certain things must shift in order for a family to become an army. First of all, a family must incorporate discipleship, equipping, and training through five-fold teaching and impartation. People must be taught not to depend solely upon the pastor to meet all their needs or be preoccupied by selfish interests and desires. They must evolve into mature ministers in their own gifts and learn how to pray for themselves and for others. They must be trained to exercise faith for their own needs and teach other members of the family to grow up and do likewise. As this happens, a paradigm shift takes place and the saints realize there is more to their church experience than needs being met. Within them evolves a sense of their divine purpose and destiny in God. They discover that their individual destiny is tied to the corporate identity, and that power released at the corporate level accomplishes more than anything that may be accomplished alone.

THEY MUST BE TRAINED TO EXERCISE FAITH FOR THEIR OWN NEEDS AND TEACH OTHER MEMBERS OF THE FAMILY TO GROW UP AND DO LIKEWISE.

Equipping and training the saints is a continual process because one never arrives in his quest to understand the awesomeness of Christ and His kingdom. However, as we evolve and mature into an army, we learn that training alone is not enough; we have to move out of the walls of "church life" and engage society as light and salt. Jesus says it like this in Matthew 5:13-16:

"You are the salt of the earth. But if the salt loses its saltiness, how can it be made salty again? It is no longer good for anything, except to be thrown out and trampled by men. You are the light of the world. A city on a hill cannot be hidden. Neither do people light a lamp and put it under a bowl. Instead they put it on its stand, and it gives light to everyone in the house. In the same way, let your light shine before men, that they may see your good deeds and praise your Father in heaven." (NIV)

OUR MISSION FIELDS HAVE TO BECOME THE ARENAS OF EVERYDAY LIFE.

Our mission fields have to become the arenas of everyday life. We have to invade and occupy the places where we work, play, shop, conduct business, and so on. We must become living epistles who reflect the Father's character and nature as we invade and occupy the areas of commerce, entertainment, government, education, and all dynamics of earth-life with the power and authority of Christ. We must attain to the high call of God for "the praise of His glory" (Eph. 1:12) and engage our divine assignments.

GOD ALWAYS INTENDED THE CHURCH TO BE AN APOSTOLIC EXPRESSION OF "SENT ONES" WHO CHANGE CULTURE THROUGH HIS POWER AND DEMONSTRATION.

In the fourth and final wheel, I saw the word *apostolic*. God spoke to me that He always intended the church to be an apostolic expression of "sent ones" who change culture through His power and demonstration. Miracles, signs, and wonders follow them as hallmarks of God's habitation within the kingdom system. As saints are trained to embrace the heart of the Father, they become fully equipped and furnished with sound biblical teaching. They then flow with the heartbeat and directive of the Holy Spirit as they invade society with the love of God and demonstrate the message of hope and faith.

PLURALITY OF LEADERSHIP IS AT THE CORE OF THE KINGDOM SYSTEM AND IS CRITICAL TO THE SUCCESS OF THE SAINTS.

Plurality of leadership is at the core of the kingdom system and is critical to the success of the saints. It involves a team concept that is firmly rooted and grounded in Christ and releases righteous governmental oversight to the saints. It also establishes accountability and a hedge of protection against leader burnout and abandonment of the assignments God gives the church. The synergy of the team-model produces a strength and momentum that can only be gained through the sum of all its parts.

Built within the team model are the unique roles of mothers and fathers in the faith, a critical component of the church. Mothers are powerful people. Though strong in spirit, it is their heart for spiritual sons and daughters that causes them to lay down their own desires and needs for the sake of the next generation. They are always there for their children and provide loving, caring support for those around them.

BUILT WITHIN THE TEAM MODEL ARE THE UNIQUE ROLES OF MOTHERS AND FATHERS IN THE FAITH, A CRITICAL COMPONENT OF THE CHURCH.

Fathers, on the other hand, seem to have an understanding of the unique nature or "bent" of the spiritual son or daughter and can provide spiritual insight into the child's destiny. Through the father's blessing, the child is affirmed, security and self esteem are instilled, and the child is empowered to prosper and succeed with the full knowledge that their father has undergirded them with his love and support. Such blessing propels them into their destiny, strengthens the father/child relationship, and perpetuates generational growth and momentum.

The emergence of patriarchal leadership in the kingdom system is in no way to be interpreted as an evidence of weakness on the mother's part in engaging in key leadership positions. It is biblically clear that women are able ministers of the Gospel and can operate in five-fold office gifts the same as men. We realize that women throughout history have demonstrated strong leadership capabilities time after time. We are simply saying that mothers and fathers operate effectively as a team when they understand their unique roles and engage the next generation accordingly.

The kingdom system is a powerful exhibit of the life of God through the demonstration of His love, goodness, power, signs, wonders, and miracles. It is displayed by healing the sick, casting out devils, praying in tongues, and fulfilling Jesus' Great Commission to "go and make disciples of all nations, baptizing them in the name of the Father and of the Son and of the Holy Spirit, and teaching them to obey everything I have commanded you. And surely I am with you always, to the very end of the age" (Matt. 28:19-20 NIV).

THE APOSTOLIC NATURE OF THE KINGDOM SYSTEM COMPELS THE FAMILY OF GOD TO MOVE OUT OF THE FOUR WALLS OF THE BUILDING WE IN AMERICA CALL "CHURCH" AND FULFILL OUR UNIQUE CALLING TO TRANSFORM CULTURE AS ABLE MINISTERS OF THE GOSPEL.

The apostolic nature of the kingdom system compels the family of God to move out of the four walls of the building we in America call "church" and fulfill our unique calling to transform culture as able ministers of the Gospel. Through demonstrating God's reign and rule, we establish thrones of righteousness and dismantle thrones of iniquity. Not only will lives change, but culture will shift as the way will be paved for future generations to gain greater spiritual ground than those before them.

The last thing I saw in the picture was a roadway and the words "changing culture" over it. I saw the wheels of family, army, and apostolic moving within one another and as they did, they went forward in one single motion on the roadway. It was obvious they were going somewhere. As I asked the Lord about this, He made it clear that the goal of the kingdom church is to change culture. She is a true invading and occupying force in the earth. Flowing as containers of the fruit and power of the Holy Spirit, she effectively engages lost and apostate humanity with the love and strength of Christ as she heralds the message of the King. Just like Paul, she demonstrates the message through the power and authority of the Holy Spirit. Spiritual resistance is torn down and sin is swallowed up with love, peace, and power.

Cultural change is evidenced by salvation as it occurs in individuals, cities, and nations. As individuals become enlightened by the Gospel message, receive Christ as Savior, and yield to His kingship, the government of God becomes established in the human heart. As this evolves from individuals to communities, the kingdom then invades all areas of society including families, civil government, educational systems, businesses, media, the entertainment industry, and so on. The Word of God once again becomes the standard by which men govern their behavior and all arenas of society are affected. The family unit regains its place of importance, the hearts of fathers and children are rightly knitted together, righteous laws are created that honor Christ, courts begin to pass righteous judgment while not legislating from the bench, and our schools, businesses, and culture become honorable and prosperous once again.

CHAPTER TWELVE

A NEW WAY

God is turning the ship at Kingdom Life. We are nowhere near where we are going to be, but we are also nowhere near where we have been. After God revealed the model for the kingdom church, I realized there were some structural changes that needed to be made in order to shift into the right direction. The first change that had to be made was in implementing proper leadership structure within the church. I clearly understood that we would not be able to build correctly under traditional pastor leadership. What was needed was a representation of all five-fold and elder gifts in the church.

WE SHIFTED OUR LEADERSHIP TEAM BY CREATING A MODEL OF FIVE-FOLD, ELDER, AND MARKETPLACE MINISTRY GIFTS THAT COMPRISED A GOVERNING BOARD AND ADVISORY BOARD.

To move forward, we needed a leadership team much like that of the Antioch church. In Acts 13, the church at Antioch was mainly undergirded by the apostles and prophets who commissioned teams of ministers to go out and build the kingdom. It was not led by one person, and it was certainly not led by a single pastor gift. It had a full expression of all the five-fold gifts working together. In much the same way, we shifted our leadership team by creating a model of five-fold, elder, and marketplace ministry gifts that comprised a governing board and advisory board.

❦❦

MEMBERS WHO EXHIBITED A SHEPHERD GIFT WERE IDENTIFIED, TRAINED, AND SET IN PLACE TO SERVE AS "PASTOR SHEPHERDS" OF THE CHURCH FAMILY.

Under this newly formed leadership team, we began to shift the dynamic of the church family. Since personal needs are almost always a top priority in families, we addressed this area first. We began recognizing each member of the body as an able minister with gifts that were essential to the health and maturity of the family. As such, members who exhibited a shepherd gift were identified, trained, and set in place to serve as "pastor shepherds" of the church family. We did not consider them as extensions of the senior pastor, but rather as shepherds according to the gift of God that was in them. Under the oversight of the leadership team, they were given full authority to minister as shepherds to the church family. For example, if someone was ill, pastor shepherds would visit the person to minister comfort and healing. If someone needed meals delivered to their home, shepherds would see that it was taken care of. If counseling needs arose, they stepped in and helped. They were released to minister in prayer during church gatherings, operate in the gifts of the Holy Spirit, and engage in body ministry without hesitation as they were led. As time has progressed, we have discovered that the less structure we give these ministers, the more genuine and powerful their ministries have become, and they have taken a place of ownership in the body.

The next shift occurred in men's and women's ministries. I cast vision to the men and women of Kingdom Life that they needed to become spiritual fathers and mothers to the young people in our body. Instead of meeting together for Bible studies and fellowships, they needed to connect with the generations and become a blessing to the youth and children.

MOTHERS AND FATHERS IN THE FAITH CAN BLESS THE NEXT GENERATION.

One of the tools we discovered to help us make this shift was Craig Hill's book *Ancient Paths*. The main theme of the book is that our identity and destiny are tied directly to the blessing of the Father. Without this blessing, we tend to flounder around in uncertainty about who we are and become noneffective in fulfilling our destiny. However, with this blessing, we can shift into the persons God has called us to be. By putting our men and women through this course, they have gained a greater understanding of how spiritual blessing is supposed to work and have started shifting into their roles as mothers and fathers in the faith who can bless the next generation.

This revelation has become so powerful that we have even implemented it as a part of our annual Advancing the

Kingdom Conference. In one of the special sessions, we invite all of our families to come forward to receive a spiritual blessing from the fathers and mothers of Kingdom Life. These individuals are couples in our body who have demonstrated the desire, maturity, and ability to father and mother the next generation. As they pray spiritual blessing over those at the conference, many experience the love of God which results in a powerful expression of affirmation, healing, and deliverance in attendees' lives.

INSTEAD OF VIEWING OUR CHILDREN AND YOUTH AS YOUNG PEOPLE ONLY, WE NOW RECOGNIZE THEM AS SONS AND DAUGHTERS.

Youth and children's ministry have also shifted as a result of the kingdom church model. Traditional youth and children's ministries have ceased to exist. Instead of viewing our children and youth as young people only, we now recognize them as sons and daughters. As offspring who represent the future hope of God's kingdom, we now seek to "father" and "mother" them rather than "teach" and "mentor" them. We have even incorporated them into our main worship service instead of segregating them into their own groups. They are given room to prophesy, share words of exhortation and encouragement, give scriptures or testimonies and even visions God has given them with the entire church family. The best part is that it is working. Young people are connecting with adults, and spiritual parenting is taking shape. The hearts of the fathers are turning to the sons, the hearts of the sons are turning to the fathers, and the church family is becoming healthier and happier.

Another shift we took was in preparing the family to become an army. This dynamic, while involving training, is nothing like the boot camp mentality of the training system. The foundation for training in the kingdom system is discipleship, not cloning. Quite surprisingly, when we launched our discipleship program at Kingdom Life, we discovered that even though many of our people had attended church most of their lives many of them had never been discipled. Accordingly, we adopted a twenty-six-week curriculum and began systematic, individualized discipleship training on a volunteer basis. Upon completion of this kind of training, each disciple is charged to disciple another, and the process is repeated (like a pyramid) until all are trained.

The next step to forming an army involved ministry training. We had been offering quarterly weekend seminars for a while, but we converted them into a monthly training school. The school is currently held during regular service times so that the entire church body can attend, and in this manner, each member of the church family has the opportunity to receive ongoing ministry training.

As a result of the new kingdom church model, we shifted deeper into our apostolic assignment. Since the birth of Kingdom Life, the apostolic dimension had always been a part of our dynamic. When the church was only a year old, my son Brandon planned and organized a citywide youth event called "Revolution" to reach the teen community of our city with the message of the Gospel. The church family rallied around the event and was able to reach out to over four hundred people on that day. It was an amazing example of what a group of people who already had an apostolic DNA working in them could do.

As we have progressed in this revelation, we have done other things to engage our apostolic assignment. I will mention the word "engage" over the next several pages to indicate connecting with and implementing the kingdom church model. One creative thing we started was closing the church every fifth Sunday of the year to send the Kingdom Life family into the marketplace to "*be* the church." We have ministered in local retirement centers, out-of-town facilities for abused boys and girls, hospitals, our neighborhoods, and have even met together in homes for Bible study, prayer, and fellowship. On these Sundays, no one is left in the church building because everyone is somewhere *being* the church. Like Elvis, we have "left the building!"

One particular Sunday, more than fifty of the church family traveled three hours away to spend three days at an East Texas farm where children are placed by Child Protective Services. On the farm are several houses, each of which has a married couple who serve as parents to the children while they recover from their abusive home situations. For three days, the church family ministered to the children and houseparents on this farm. We rebuilt bathrooms, remodeled houses, painted rooms, sewed and hung drapes, as well as ministered one-on-one to the children and staff. It was a glorious time. Never before had I seen our church family so engaged in a kingdom endeavor. The event was so powerful that we have continued to talk about it to this day.

As our revelation of the kingdom church model continues to unfold, we seek new and improved ways of being the church and impacting the culture around us. Most recently, we have partnered with a ministry couple in the body who minister to the homeless. Each Saturday the Kingdom Life family joins them to feed 150 homeless people in the city of Dallas. Testimonies come back each week of salvations, deliverances, and spiritual breakthroughs in the lives of the people. Many of them are getting back on their feet—finding jobs and reentering the world again as productive citizens. It has been such a blessing to be a part of this culture-changing endeavor.

Our church family also currently engages in international missions. To date, we have traveled to the nations of Vietnam, Ecuador, Costa Rica, and Mexico to train ministers, encourage the body of Christ, evangelize the lost, and preach the Gospel of the kingdom. Adults, youth, and children alike engage in these missions and minister side by side. We have seen God do miracles on these trips—the sick have been healed, the crippled have walked, the oppressed have been set free, and even the dead have been raised to life again.

Once while Brandon was ministering in a youth crusade in 2007, a boy was found in an unresponsive state outside the pavilion where the meeting was being held. Another child had found him and ran into the meeting to get help. One of the workers happened to be a medical doctor, and she and other workers immediately ran to the child, only to discover that he was indeed dead. The doctor immediately called for medical help as she initiated CPR. Because of my experience as a nurse, I stood close by to help. In spite of prolonged CPR efforts, the child was not responding. Immediately, the crusade workers who had gathered around the boy began to pray. They commanded life to come back into his body, and, as they prayed, he suddenly gasped and returned to life. I personally witnessed the boy take his first breath. The doctor immediately stopped CPR and later verified that it was a true miracle. The ambulance arrived and transported the boy to the hospital, but by the time he arrived, he was perfectly whole. They examined him, and finding nothing wrong, sent him home. Once again, I witnessed the kingdom in action as the church took her rightful place in culture.

Kingdom Life engages culture in even more ways. We are getting involved in civil government. Awhile back, Brandon, Kathy, and I had an opportunity to meet with the mayor of our city. We were well received, and the meeting turned into a discussion about what we could do to help the mayor take care of our city's needs. Almost jokingly he told us, "Pray for rain." You see, our state had been in a severe drought for more than eighteen months, and our water supply was severely depleted. It was so bad that some of the area lake levels were down by as much as eighteen feet, requiring residents to ration city water. The mayor told us the city had plenty of storage tanks and a recently installed superstructure to collect all the necessary water, but unfortunately, we needed rain to fill them up. He related that he had sent an e-mail to some local pastors asking them to pray for rain but wanted to know if we could pray as well. We promised the mayor that our Tuesday prayer group would make this our number-one priority and started praying right away.

Taking this very seriously, we immediately started praying for rain. We knew the gravity of the situation and prayed week after week for God to open the heavens and let the rain fall. Nothing happened for a while, but one day, the sky opened up, and it began to rain. It didn't just rain—it poured day after day for months. By the time it finally stopped, not only were our area lakes filled to capacity, but every lake in Texas was overflowing. It was amazing to see what God did. He answered our prayers in a huge way.

A few months later, my son Brandon was eating lunch at a local restaurant when the mayor happened to walk in. As he approached, Brandon almost jokingly asked if he wanted our church to stop praying for rain. The mayor replied, "Never stop praying for rain. We can always use it. Just pray that it won't come all at once." Brandon laughed and then asked the mayor if there was anything else our church could pray for. He immediately gave us another assignment, and we continue to engage it to this day. In doing so, we feel that we are a part of the kingdom in action.

A final dynamic of our current apostolic assignment is providing spiritual oversight to ordained ministers in covenant relationship with us. These ministers are involved in apostolic training centers, local churches, mission bases and also engage in marketplace ministry. Part of our responsibility to them is making sure they receive proper spiritual covering and undergirding from the ministry. It is a blessing to work with these mighty men and women of God as they engage the kingdom for cultural transformation of their cities, regions, and nations.

As the Kingdom Life family continues to grow and develop, we are becoming an army that is better trained and equipped. We are impacting culture for the King of kings, and we believe the best is yet to come. I feel like we've finally pulled around the box truck and are on our way up the highway to fulfilling our destiny and pointing the world toward Jesus. These are exciting times indeed!

CHAPTER THIRTEEN

THE ROAD AHEAD

Now that you have read this book, my sincere hope and desire is that you have discovered a new key to unlocking your destiny in God. Maybe you were able to identify with the pastor system and have found yourself stuck in a "me-centered" environment that is producing a lack of fulfillment, frustration, or burnout in your life. Maybe you are pastoring a group of people who look to you for their every need, and you are realizing it will never be possible to accomplish this great feat. Maybe you've created dozens of programs and activities in your church to keep the saints busy, but you are feeling exhausted as you feed the machine week after week to keep everything going. Maybe you are the person sitting in the pew disillusioned and dissatisfied with American Christianity, and you want something more.

Maybe you are the person who's stuck in the training system and paralyzed by your leader. You're living in constant fear of disappointing your leader and not measuring up to the standard that he or she has set for you. Maybe you've done all the right things and said all the right words, but you simply feel like it's not enough. You feel like you'll never obtain the mark set before you, and week after week, you feel like a failure in your walk with the Lord.

Maybe for you, the training system has gone even one step further and you find yourself a victim of it. Maybe your leader is spiritually abusing you, manipulating you, or controlling you. Maybe your leader is abusive or misusing authority to force you to do things against your will. Maybe you've been affected by some of the abuses of authority and did not even realize it was wrong. Maybe you're trapped in this system, and you're screaming on the inside, *I want out*, but you don't know where the answer lies.

Well, I'm here to tell you today there is an answer. There is a way out. You don't have to remain in either one of these systems if you don't want to. You can be free through God's kingdom.

The kingdom of God is liberating. It is life. It is peace. It is joy. It is God's answer. When *He* reigns over all, everything comes into perfect alignment. There is no disorder in His kingdom. There is no abuse in His kingdom. There is no bondage in His kingdom. The Bible says in 2 Corinthians 3:17, "Where the Spirit of the Lord is, there is liberty." This means that wherever God is allowed to reign and rule, there is an abundance of every good thing. For instance, God is the Healer, so wherever He is allowed to reign and rule, there is health. God is the Deliverer, so wherever He is allowed to reign and rule, there is freedom. God is the Redeemer, so wherever He is allowed to reign and rule, there is redemption. This principle applies to everything in creation, everything in humanity, and everything in culture.

The application of this truth is such: If you *truly* want to see things change inside you and around you, you must allow His kingdom to come and His will to be done in your heart. When this happens, everything in your life will shift.

Nothing will remain the same. He will release His glory—the essence of who He is—and everything negative that comes into contact with it will be swallowed up. Destructive mind-sets will yield to the life of God, and negative thought patterns will conform to His way of thinking. This is the kingdom of God in action.

IF YOU *TRULY* WANT TO SEE THINGS CHANGE INSIDE YOU AND AROUND YOU, YOU MUST ALLOW HIS KINGDOM TO COME AND HIS WILL TO BE DONE IN YOUR HEART.

The choice is yours. You can stay behind the box truck, stuck in old systems that produce death, or you can move around the truck by choosing life. You can allow His kingdom to come into your life. All you have to do is say, "Lord, I want out of this system. I'm tired of the systems of man. I'm tired of meaningless Christianity. I'm tired of going to church on Sunday while I watch the world around me disintegrate on Monday. I'm exhausted with feeding the machine called church. I'm tired of trying to keep everyone happy and believing that my calling is tied to how large I can grow my box. God, I'm tired of the box. I've put You in a box. I've put myself in a box. I've put everyone around me in a box. It's time to step out of the box. It's time for You to come and do what You want to do and that's to build Your kingdom inside of me. Thank you that this is a new day. Thank you that this is a new hour. Thank you that You are shifting the American church. Thank you that I'm a part of that shift. Show me how to take the next step. Show me how to let Your kingdom come in my life. Show me Your ways. Show me Your heart. Show me Your kingship. I'm ready. I'm hungry. I'm stepping out. In Jesus' name. Amen."

If you just prayed that prayer, I believe you're ready to shift around the box truck. I believe you're ready for change and ready to become a kingdom person. So what's the next step?

Find other kingdom people. Connect with kingdom-minded churches, ministries, and networks. Pray for a spiritual father or mother in the faith who understands the kingdom and can impart its principles and dynamics into your life. Study the word "kingdom" in the Bible. Ask God to show you the pattern of the kingdom through both Old and New Testaments. Buy books and CDs on the kingdom and digest their contents (we have provided a list of other kingdom resources in the back of this book). Dive into these resources; let them sink into your heart and transform your way of thinking.

Finally, put what you learn into action. The kingdom is built one person at a time, one group at a time, one region at a time, one culture at a time, and one nation at a time. Allow God to show you where you fit in the kingdom and start fulfilling the assignments He gives you. Step by step, little by little, you will start to discover God's kingdom at work within you, and you will be forever changed. Start today. The kingdom is waiting for you!

Alcorn, Randy. *Heaven.* Wheaton, IL: Tyndale House Publishers, 2004.

Enlow, Johnny. *The Seven Mountain Prophecy.* Lake Mary, FL: Creation House, 2008.

Freed, Sandie. *Strategies from Heaven's Throne: Claiming the Life God Wants for You.* Grand Rapids, MI: Chosen Books, 2007.

Hamon, Bill. *The Day of the Saints.* Shippensburg, PA: Destiny Image Publishers, Inc., 2002.

Hodges, Jim. *Releasing the Sounds of Heaven on Earth: Aligning the Church's Worship with Kingdom Revelation.* Denton, TX: Glory of Zion International Ministries, 2004.

Jacobs, Cindy. *The Reformation Manifesto.* Bloomington, MN: Bethany House Publishers, 2008.

Johnson, Bill and Vallotton. *The Supernatural Ways of Royalty: Discovering Your Rights and Privileges of Being a Son or Daughter of God.* Shippensburg, PA: Destiny Image Publishers, Inc., 2006.

Munroe, Myles. *Advancing the Kingdom: Understanding God's Priority and Primary Interest.* Shippensburg, PA: Destiny Image Publishers, Inc., 2007.

Munroe, Myles. *Rediscovering the Kingdom: Ancient Hope for Our 21st Century World.* Shippensburg, PA: Destiny Image Publishers, 2004.

Pierce, Chuck D. *God's Unfolding Battle Plan*. Denton, TX: Glory of Zion International Ministries, 2008.

Pierce, Chuck D. *Interpreting the Times*. Lake Mary, FL: Charisma House, 2008.

Sheets, Dutch, and Chuck D. Pierce. *Releasing the Prophetic Destiny of a Nation*. Shippensburg, PA: Destiny Image Publishers, 2005.

Wagner, C. Peter. *Dominion! How Kingdom Action Can Change the World*. Grand Rapids, MI: Chosen Books, 2008.

Wentroble, Barbara. *Praying With Authority*. Ventura, CA: Regal Books, 2003.

Yoder, Barbara. *The Breaker Anointing*. Ventura, CA: Regal Books, 2004.

ABOUT THE AUTHOR

Larry Burden has been in full-time ministry for over two decades. Called to ministry in 1987, he was the founder and pastor of a local church in Texas until moving to California in 1992 to attend Bible college. Following the completion of his ministry training, he and his wife Kathy joined the staff of a newly established church where they served as the associate pastors. During their more than seven-year tenure as associate pastors, they each taught courses in the Bible school, ministered in the church, and traveled to more than forty nations preaching and teaching the Gospel of Jesus Christ.

Larry has a desire to see the kingdom of God established in the heart of every Christian believer. His ministry blends the stability of the Word of God, the strength of the Holy Spirit, and the love of the Father to bring a refreshing word of life and hope to the body of Christ. As a servant in God's kingdom, Larry's ministry focuses upon shifting the local church into a kingdom mind-set in order to impact society at every level for the kingdom of God.

The Burdens currently reside in Frisco, Texas, where they serve as founders of Kingdom Life International, Inc. and as pastors of Kingdom Life Christian Center. They are ordained through the Federation of Ministers and Churches International and are the directors of Kingdom Life Ministerial Alliance. Larry may be contacted at:

Larry Burden
Kingdom Life International, Inc.
P.O. Box 1749
Frisco, TX 75034
214-618-1500
www.kingdomlife.org